The Confessions of Saint Augustine

THE CONFESSIONS OF SAINT AUGUSTINE

An Annotated Bibliography of Modern Criticism, 1888–1995

Richard Severson

Bibliographies and Indexes in Religious Studies,
Number 40
G. E. Gorman, Advisory Editor

GREENWOOD PRESS
Westport, Connecticut • London

Library of Congress Cataloging-in-Publication Data

Severson, Richard James, 1955–
    The confessions of Saint Augustine : an annotated bibliography of
modern criticism, 1888–1995 / Richard Severson.
        p.   cm .— (Bibliographies and indexes in religious studies,
ISSN 0742–6836 ; no. 40)
    Includes bibliographical references and index.
    ISBN 0–313–29995–1 (alk. paper)
    1. Augustine, Saint, Bishop of Hippo. Confessiones—Bibliography.
I. Title. II. Series.
Z8047.7.S47   1996
[BR65.A62]
016.2702′092—dc20   96–9465

British Library Cataloguing in Publication Data is available.

Library of Congress Catalog Card Number: 96–9465
ISBN: 0–313–29995–1
ISSN: 0742–6836

First published in 1996

Greenwood Press, 88 Post Road West, Westport, CT 06881
An imprint of Greenwood Publishing Group, Inc.

Printed in the United States of America

10 9 8 7 6 5 4 3 2

Contents

Series Foreword

[Augustine] had long felt a distaste towards the 'vanities' of which he accuses himself in the *Confessions*... his licentious desires and indulgences; his courtship of influential friends who might find him a 'prefectship'; his search for a rich wife who would not prove a financial responsibility; his craving for respite from the stress of teaching.

Kenneth Kirk, *The Vision of God*

The function of theology as critical reflection on praxis has gradually become more clearly defined in recent years, but it has its roots in the first centuries of the Church's life. The Augustinian theology of history which we find in *The City of God*, for example, is based on a true analysis of the signs of the times and the demands with which they challenge the Christian community.

Gustavo Gutierrez, *A Theology of Liberation*

As Kenneth Kirk reminds us in *The Vision of God*, Augustine is a very modern man, baring his soul and describing his anxieties, his shortcomings and carnal desires. From Augustine's *Confessions* we know more about him than almost any other figure in late antiquity. His weaknesses, and particularly his self-exposed sexual escapades, have endeared him to generations of Christians and non-Christians alike—he speaks to us "where we are" rather than from some other, purer plane of existence that we associate with most of the Early Fathers. Indeed, through the *Confessions* St. Augustine appears to be the most accessible and the most human of all the Fathers, and for this reason is perhaps the best loved. Yet he was not just a converted sinner whose existential writings continue to resound meaningfully in the personal lives of believers. Rather, he was a prodigious writer (eleven substantial volumes in the Latin edition of the Maurists) on a range of topics that have significantly defined the parameters of Christian theology then and now. Furthermore, he articulated a number of key doctrinal positions that have been accepted as normative in traditional Christianity for centuries—including the doctrine of original sin, the place of the church in the world, and believers' dependence on divine grace. Without

Augustine's formative influence on these and other important theological issues, Western Christianity would not be as we know it today.

The scope of Augustine's influence, and the doctrines he articulated, can be seen most succinctly in his responses to three great controversies of his era— Manichaeism, and the doctrine of original sin; Donatism, and the concept of the church in the world; Pelagianism, and the necessity for divine grace in human endeavour. Beginning with Manichaeism, Augustine's articulation of the doctrine of original sin was in response to Mani's teaching that humans are basically rational and spiritual beings created by God but housed in physical bodies created by an evil demiurge. For St. Augustine original sin was a far more legitimate explanation for the appearance of evil in the midst of God's good creation. He was thus the first theologian to incorporate a theory of the Fall in the essential doctrines of the Christian faith and to articulate its meaning for humanity. Specifically, he came to locate sin and evil in the human will. After the Fall this will turned away from its focus on God to an inward concentration on the self; evil thus stems from a will that has lost its attraction to God and seeks its own happiness in various ways. This divided will restlessly seeks happiness until God's grace intervenes and the individual ceases his self-seeking satisfaction. Evil is thus temporary and originates in the human will, which is a clear contrast to the Manichean description of evil as necessary and permanent.

In the Donatist schism issues of ecclesiology and sacramental theology were at stake. The Donatists taught that the true, "pure" church was a limited society of the holy, separated and distinct from surrounding society by virtue of the sacraments that were dispensed by clergy who were aloof from cooperation with the state, which after all was a persecutor of Christians. For Augustine, however, the church was not some holy bride of Christ placed on a pedestal but rather the wheat among the chaff, a strong and confident association that was able to assimilate and change secular culture without itself becoming diluted by secularism. The Donatists also taught that sacraments administered by "imperfect" priests were not only invalid but actually harmful to their recipients. In response, Augustine formulated a sacramental theology that viewed the sacraments as given by Christ rather than by a priest, and therefore not dependent on the goodness or otherwise of Christ's representatives on earth. In dealing with the Donatists Augustine thus constructed a theology of the church as an institution consisting of well-meaning humans who would achieve perfection only in the City of God that would emerge as the final resurrection, but bolstered in this world by efficacious sacraments from Christ.

The third controversy, Pelagianism, allowed Augustine to advance his views on original sin and grace, and to articulate a doctrine of predestination. Pelagius and his followers maintained that it was possible for believers to achieve Christian perfection in the present, and that true Christians in fact were obligated to strive for perfection in this life. In the Pelagian view original sin was replaced by something closer to unfortunate habits engendered by misdirected, worldly values that could be overcome by human effort. For Augustine human effort was important, but was also in vain without the benefit of God's enabling grace granted to individuals in different measure according to some divine plan. Because of original sin, divine grace is necessary to restore a right relationship to God.

Divine grace, life in the community of the Church, the value of sacramental participation, the debilitating nature of original sin—all of this from one person, who also led a full and active life as a bishop. Is it any wonder, then, that St. Augustine the man and Augustinian theology have enjoyed such a following over the centuries, and have inspired so many historians and theologians to a lifetime of study? Over many decades their study has resulted in a massive corpus of Augustiniana. In just twenty-five years, for example, there have been at least three major biographies of Augustine: Van der Meer's *Augustine the Biship* (1961), Peter Brown's *Augustine of Hippo* (1967), Henry Chadwick's *Augustine* (1986). And the range of articles and monographs devoted to his theology beggars quantification: a perusal of such major bibliographies as Andresen's *Bibliographia Augustiniana* or van Bavel's *Répertoire Bibliographique de Saint Augustin* reminds us of the prodigious output of the Augustiniana industry. We have works from theologians and classicists, literary critics and psychologists, historians and social scientists, ethicists and biblical scholars, all adding their interpretations to the corpus.

But while interest spans all the works of St. Augustine, it is the *Confessions* more than any other writing that continue to capture popular imagination and serious scholarship. Speaking of Augustine's writings in general, Van der Meer maintains that "no one has ever caused more shock, aroused more religious feeling and more ardent enthusiasm for God's honour and the salvation of souls, through his books and sermons, that Augustine."[1] He could just as well have limited his remarks to the *Confessions*, which since Adolf von Harnack's seminal lecture in 1888 have attracted almost phenomenal interest. As Richard Severson suggests in the opening chapter of the present volume, it is studied by literary critics as the paradigmatic Western autobiography, by psychologists as an ancient case study, by philosophers as a tract on time, and by theologians for many reasons. To help provide some guidance through this ever-growing body of literature, it was thus most appropriate to receive from Dr. Severson of the Shoen Library at Marylhurst College in Oregon a proposal for a volume devoted to the *Confessions* of St. Augustine.

With a doctorate in theology and a professional degree in library science, Dr. Severson clearly possesses the skills and knowledge needed to gather and evaluate the literature on Augustine's *Confessions*—this is clearly evident in his judicious choice of entries and the quality of annotations in the bibliography. Moreover, his introductory essay, "Modern Criticism of the *Confessions*," clearly sets forth the principal themes that have emerged in the last hundred years of scholarly study, and this analysis is carefully cross-referenced to entries in the bibliography. Students new to the study of the *Confessions*, as well as scholars seeking to extend or update their knowledge, will find this discussion of particular value. Furthermore, the bibliography itself succeeds in covering, in its eight specific subject categories, all key themes related to the *Confessions*: autobiography, literary criticism, conversion experience, philosophy, psychology, spirituality, textual unity, theological issues. In these sections the compiler has thoroughly and objectively annotated a fully representative range of the most important anglophone works on the *Confessions*. Indeed, so extensive is the treatment (extending to some 468 items) that the bibliography must be regarded as an indispensable resource not only for newcomers to the subject but also for those engaged in advanced study and scholarship in a range of disciplines.

Putting this volume together has been no simple task for the compiler, yet he has done so competently and in record time—to the extent that my role as Advisory Editor of the series has been predominantly a passive one. The result is a carefully structured and judicious survey that is accessible to students and useful to scholars. *The Confessions of St. Augustine: An Annotated Bibliography of Modern Criticism, 1888-1995* sets a high standard in the bibliographic treatment of St. Augustine and his writings, and I am pleased to welcome it as a most important addition to Bibliographies and Indexes in Religious Studies. Heretofore this series has followed a largely thematic approach in its topics, looking for instance at ecology and Christian faith, human rights in Judaism, death and dying. Dr. Severson's volume takes a different tack, focusing on the work of a single individual; it is hoped that subsequent volumes might extend this to other leaders and thinkers in any religious tradition.

---

[1] F. Van der Meer. *Augustine the Bishop: The Life and Work of a Father of the Church.* Trans. by Brian Battershaw and G.R. Lamb (London: Sheed and Ward, 1961), p. 581.

Dr. G.E. Gorman, FLA FRSA
Advisory Editor
Charles Sturt University—Riverina
September 1996

Preface

This book is intended to guide English speaking scholars and students through the maze of modern *Confessions* interpretation. The breadth of interest in this ancient text over the past century is remarkable: theologians, classicists, historians, philosophers, psychologists, and literary critics have all laid claim to the *Confessions*. It is a unique classic of world literature and Western Christianity.

The book is organized into nine chapters. The first chapter provides a critical introduction to *Confessions* scholarship, and the remaining chapters constitute the bibliography proper. Two of the eight bibliography chapters are devoted to literary criticism of the *Confessions*: one to the growing subdiscipline of autobiographical studies, one to more traditional literary (and historical) analysis. There are chapters on philosophical, psychological, and theological issues raised by interpreters of the *Confessions*. Another chapter is devoted solely to studies of Augustine's famous conversion narrative in Book VIII of the *Confessions*. Finally, there are chapters pertaining to the classical status of the *Confessions*, and to its structural unity as a text.

The scope is limited to scholarly studies of the *Confessions* written in English between the years 1888 and 1995. Most of the studies are articles or books specifically written about the *Confessions*. These materials were selected from bibliographies, library catalogs, and standard periodical indexes. Also included are articles and books that either significantly depend upon the *Confessions* in their constructive arguments or offer brief but important interpretive remarks about the *Confessions*. Selection of these less obvious materials was based upon their presence and significance in the primary *Confessions* literature. Also included are a few French works of undoubted significance that are readily available in good American libraries (*see*: **078, 082, 153, 166-67**). Accessible Ph.D. dissertations from American and Canadian universities are included; non-Ph.D. level theses and papers are not included.

Two types of cross referencing are employed throughout the bibliography. First, some of the annotations make cross references to other relevant items in the bibliography. Second, lists of cross references are included under most of the headings within each chapter. These references lead the reader to works of a somewhat similar nature that are found elsewhere.

Three indexes are included. There is an index of authors and editors, an index of titles, and an extensive subject index.

Acknowledgments

I wish to thank Dr. Jan Marie Fortier, library director at Marylhurst College, for making the resources and services of Shoen Library available for my use. I could not have finished this project without the cheerful assistance of Kris Simpson, Sean Gutmann, and B.J. Andersen from the interlibrary loan department. I also wish to thank Father Hugh Feiss, library director at Mt. Angel Abbey, for providing me with office space at a first class theological library. Paula Hamilton and Darlene Strand made Benedictine hospitality a pleasant reality in my frequent visits to the Abbey. Finally, I want to acknowledge a grateful student's debt to Dr. Carl Orgren, who introduced me to the world and work of bibliography.

1

Modern Criticism of the *Confessions*

By the late nineteenth century the forces that created modernity (science, religious and philosophical criticism, historical consciousness, democratic liberties, romantic individualism, industrialization) had forged the distinctive mindset of the modern scholar. Like René Descartes, the modern scholar entertains doubts about established truths; and, like Isaac Newton, the modern scholar looks to experience as the most reliable authority. Perhaps never before in human memory has such a self-confident spirit of criticism been established.

Sensational new disciplines such as Freudian psychoanalysis were created when the new scholarly perspective was brought to bear upon the study of human nature. Probably no less sensational was the quest for the historical Jesus which resulted from modern critical study of the Bible. Did Jesus ever really exist? This kind of jarring question, first raised in the nineteenth century, indicates the cultural power entailed in the modern critical spirit. Nothing is safe from criticism or left unchanged by its gaze.

In 1888 Adolf von Harnack (**170**) and Gaston Boissier (**167**) began studying St. Augustine's *Confessions* from the perspective of modern scholarly criticism. Like the Bible, the *Confessions* is an ancient religious text. Augustine wrote the *Confessions* in 397 and 398 AD, just after becoming bishop of Hippo, a small North African city. Both Harnack and Boissier questioned the truthfulness of Augustine's conversion narrative in Book VIII of the *Confessions*. Did he really hear an angelic voice under a fig tree in Milan as he said he did? Or is his story contrived for literary and persuasive purposes? Here we see modern scholarship begin to bring its doubter's spirit to bear upon Augustine's text. How the *Confessions* has fared under critical scrutiny over the past century is what this book is about. To say that it has fared well would be an understatement; it has thrived and grown in stature like few other Western classics.

The *Confessions* has thrived in the era of modern scholarship for several reasons. First, Augustine's psychological self-analysis is more in character with a modern sensibility. The same can be said about Augustine's autobiographical writing style, which was uncommon prior to the nineteenth century. For his psychological insight and for the invention of full-blown autobiography, Augustine has often been called the first modern person.

Second, Augustine's extensive influence upon medieval life and culture has become a fascinating subject for critical study. One of the ironic purposes of modern scholarship is to overcome alienation from the past that is partly a consequence of modern criticism (hence the irony). It is a new world we live in, yet there is real curiosity about what life was like before modern invention and criticism changed (seemingly) everything. Surprisingly, perhaps, the *Confessions* has proved to be one of the truly great cultural classics, comparable in its influence and ubiquity to the epics of Homer, the dialogues of Plato, and the Bible.

Third, Augustine's example as a religious and philosophical thinker has been vigorously studied. Ludwig Wittgenstein's influential *Philosophical Investigations* (**273**), for example, begins with a quotation from the *Confessions*. The *Confessions* is a window into the mind of a great thinker, a mind that has been especially valued over the past century. Augustine's theory of time, found in Book XI of the *Confessions*, is considered a philosophical masterpiece.

Due in part to the efforts of modern scholars, the *Confessions* of St. Augustine continues to grow as a classic of world literature and Western Christianity. Let me be more specific about the story of how Augustine's text has fared in its confrontation with modern criticism by previewing the chapters that are to follow in this bibliography. Each chapter focuses on one topical area of modern *Confessions* scholarship.

AUTOBIOGRAPHICAL STUDIES

The German philosopher Wilhelm Dilthey (**026**) observed that the study of autobiography would enable historians and others to develop a deeper understanding of human life categories. Dilthey's son-in-law, Georg Misch, followed up on that observation and authored a multi-volume history of autobiography. Only the first two volumes have been translated into English (**052**). Misch's work, which he began publishing in 1907, was the first scholarly study of autobiography as a distinctive genre of literature. Naturally, Misch devoted considerable attention to Augustine's *Confessions* in his account of the early history of autobiography.

Karl Weintraub is an American historian who wrote a book of some influence that also charts the history of autobiography (**045**). Unlike Misch, Weintraub assumes that the *Confessions* is the first true autobiography (many partial autobiographies predate it, as Misch's work tends to over-emphasize). Interpreting key autobiographies from Western history, Weintraub argues that individualism is strictly a modern phenomenon. This practice of employing the study of autobiographies such as the *Confessions* in order to make claims about human selfhood, first suggested by Dilthey, has become common in English language scholarship. *See:* **037-40, 042-44**.

The *Confessions* has also been a favorite for comparative analysis with other famous autobiographies. Winston Van Horne, for example, compares the *Confessions* to Malcolm X's *Autobiography* (**021**). Comparisons are also made to Rousseau's *Confessions* (**001, 006, 010-11, 040**), Petrarch's *Canzoniere* (**002, 005, 023**), Wordsworth's *Prelude* (**004, 006, 010-11**), and many others.

Canadian critic Northrop Frye (**028**), like Dilthey, made cryptic suggestions that stimulated others to study autobiography as a unique literary genre. Frye suggested that autobiography is comparable to the novel. Ever since, scholars have been trying to pinpoint the distinctive nature of autobiographical literature. Geoffrey Harpham argues that the purpose of autobiographies such as the *Confessions* is to convert life into language (**030**); Kenneth Steinhauser maintains that they constitute an act of self-invention (**034**). *See also*: **025, 027, 029, 031-33**.

What, if anything, distinguishes religious confessions from nonreligous autobiographies? This is a question that has been given considerable attention in recent studies of the *Confessions*. For example, Janet Gunn argues that the religious significance of Augustine's text is its determining feature (**062**). The desire to bear testimony to God is the structuring principle of the *Confessions* according to Jamie Scott (**067**). *See also*: **056, 058, 060, 063-64, 066**.

CLASSICAL AND LITERARY SCHOLARSHIP

Pierre Courcelle is often acknowledged as the greatest *Confessions* scholar of the century. Unfortunately, his two master works (**082, 153**) have not been translated into English. In one case (**082**), Courcelle investigates both the literary antecedents of the *Confessions*, and its literary legacy. These two questions (about the literature and culture that influenced Augustine when he wrote the *Confessions*, and about the influence his work had upon later authors and culture) have been important in English language scholarship as well.

Apart from biblical and philosophical influences discussed elsewhere, Virgil's *Aeneid* seems to be the most significant literary antecedent of the *Confessions*. Camille Bennett (**079**), Andrew Fichter (**083**), John O'Meara (**086-87**), and Carol Ramage (**090**) have all written about Augustine's use of Virgil. Joseph Pucci, on the other hand, analyzes a literary allusion to Horace's *Odes* (**089**). *See also*: **080-81, 085, 281**.

Meyer Abrams's classic study of romanticism (**091**) is an example of scholarship that depicts the influence of the *Confessions* on later culture and literature. Abrams claims that romantics such as Wordsworth secularized many of the religious ideas and themes found in the *Confessions*.

The influence of the *Confessions* upon medieval culture and literature has been discussed in a variety of contexts: John Fleming claims that the *Confessions* appears as a "supertextual" presence in a poem of Jean de Meun's (**095**); Brian McGuire refers to the determining influence of the *Confessions* as he probes the sexual orientation of Aelred of Rievaulx (**101**); and Susan Shwartz defends Geoffrey of Monmouth's *Historia* by comparing it to the *Confessions* (**106**). *See also*: **092-93, 097-98, 105, 108, 110**.

At one cutting edge of literary criticism is the attempt to "deconstruct" classics such as the *Confessions*. Deconstruction, or post-structuralism, is a form of interpretation in which many of the cultural presuppositions of a text are challenged or subverted even while the text itself is preserved and valued. Margaret Ferguson, for instance, reads the *Confessions* deconstructively by contending that Augustine's pessimistic view of language is a consequence of a basic metaphysical orientation in Western thought (**114**). This orientation implies that whatever is present for human use or observation will always be an imperfect substitute for something hidden and unattainable (human words are an imperfect substitute for the Word). Getting out from under that kind of cultural legacy, embedded in the way we think and speak, is the purpose of deconstruction. *See also*: **113, 116-17, 121, 124.**

Since it would not be possible to write about Augustine's life without interacting with his autobiography, several exemplary biographies are included in this chapter of the bibliography. Peter Brown's masterful treatment of Augustine's personality and times is particularly noteworthy (**128**). Aimé Solignac's influential "Introduction" to the *Confessions* (**078**), written in French, is also included because it provides the best mid-century review of modern (mostly French and German) scholarship. Michael Gorman's lone English language article on the manuscript tradition of the *Confessions* is included as well (**076**).

CONVERSION EXPERIENCE

Modern *Confessions* criticism began with a controversy known as the "two Augustine's theory." The theory suggests that Augustine presents two different versions of his state of mind in 386 AD. In Book VIII of the *Confessions*, written more than ten years after 386, he describes a troubling internal debate that ended in a dramatic Christian conversion. Yet in several philosophical treatises known as the Cassiciacum dialogues, written at the time in question, Augustine appears untroubled and completely absorbed by Neoplatonism. Harnack (**170**) and Boissier (**167**) noticed this apparent discrepancy in 1888, and concluded that Augustine's conversion scene must be contrived in some sense. (Others had noticed the difference prior to 1888, but had not been inclined to question Augustine's veracity.) Prosper Alfaric brought the controversy to a head in 1918 (**166**) when he argued that Augustine was actually converted to Neoplatonism in 386, not Christianity as he claims in the *Confessions*.

Two different issues are at stake in the two Augustine's controversy. One issue pertains to the historical accuracy of the *Confessions*. Was Augustine being truthful in his description of the conversion at Milan? Or was he trying to stir up his readers by employing dramatic fictional techniques? The great Courcelle (**153**) and a few others have argued for a fiction thesis: Augustine intentionally fictionalized his story for dramatic purposes. Leo Ferrari has devoted his career to making that argument in English language scholarship (**154-59**). Unlike Alfaric, and to a lesser extent Courcelle, Ferrari does not question Augustine's honesty, however. Another important English language scholar, John O'Meara, has argued against Courcelle's fiction thesis (**162**). Most scholars would probably acknowledge Augustine's flair for the dramatic, but stop well short of asserting that the *Confessions* is fiction. *See also*: **152, 160-61, 175**.

The second issue pertains to differences between Neoplatonism and Christianity, which are subtle and easily overblown. In the *Confessions,* Augustine says that he never would have understood God in a properly Christian sense without Neoplatonism. Differences between the two perspectives were mostly inconsequential in his day, but this was not so at the turn of the twentieth century, when Alfaric accused Augustine of being a falsehearted Neoplatonist. The trend to question Augustine's conversion to Christianity has been discounted by Benjamin Warfield (**183**), W. Simpson (**181**), Paul Henry (**171**), Mary Garvey (**169**), and O'Meara (**178**) in English language scholarship. Garvey's dissertation provides an excellent review of the earliest literature concerning this problem. Her conclusion, that Augustine was a true Christian in 386 AD even though he liked to use Neoplatonic language, would probably still hold today with most scholars. *See also*: **168, 172-74, 176-77, 182**.

Modern scholars have also studied the *Confessions* as a model for understanding what happens in the process of conversion. Harold Coward (**142**) claims that previously memorized scriptures came to mind when Augustine was troubled, thus enabling him to "hear" God calling him back. On the other hand, Judith Stark (**149**) analyzes the different stages that Augustine's will moved through in his transformation. Finally, Augustine's conversion narrative is occasionally contrasted with the conversion narratives of Blaise Pascal (**134, 139**), St. Paul (**135**), Samuel Coleridge (**137**), and others. *See also*: **141, 146, 148, 150-51**.

TIME AND OTHER PHILOSOPHICAL ISSUES

Augustine's discussion of time and eternity in Book XI of the *Confessions* is considered one of the most original interpretations of time ever written. According to Augustine, time is a distention of the soul backward as memory and forward as expectation. No one had formulated such an exclusively psychological theory prior to Augustine. Aristotle, in contrast, said that time pertains to the motion of physical bodies. A number of scholars have compared Augustine's theory of time with theories of other ancient thinkers. John Callahan (**236**) compares the views of Plato, Aristotle, Plotinus, and Augustine. He believes that most modern thinking about time can be traced back to one of these four philosophers. Catherine Rau (**258**) claims that Augustine's theory of time is the most advanced theory of the ancient world, anticipating Kant's transcendentalism and Einstein's relativity. *See also*: **237, 243-44, 246, 251, 254-55, 264, 266, 268**.

Other scholars have compared Augustine's views of time with modern thinkers. Several of this type entail comparisons with Wittgenstein, who himself remarked about Augustine's discussion of time (**272-73**). Seale Doss (**240**) claims that Wittgenstein's grammatical interpretation of time, based upon criticisms of Augustine, inaugurated a Copernican revolution. James McEvoy, on the other hand, defends Augustine against Wittgenstein's criticisms (**250**). *See also*: **234, 241, 265**.

Still other scholars have analyzed the particulars of Augustine's thinking about time. For example, Donald Ross (**261**) explains how Augustine could claim that time is both real and nothing more than a mental state. *See also*: **239, 247-49, 252-53, 259, 267, 269, 271**.

More research has been devoted to Augustine's treatise on time than to any other topic concerning the *Confessions*. Of almost equal interest has been the question of Neoplatonic influence upon Augustine, first broached above in the "Conversion Experience" section. Here the issue is not whether Augustine was converted to Neoplatonism rather than Christianity in 386 AD; instead, it concerns the question of which Neoplatonist thinkers Augustine actually studied. In Book VII of the *Confessions* Augustine says that he came under the influence of certain "Platonic books" while at Milan. There has been considerable debate about which books (and which authors) he means. The ongoing disagreement between Robert O'Connell and Frederick Van Fleteren represents the best of this debate in English language scholarship.

For more than thirty years O'Connell has been arguing that Plotinus was the Neoplatonist philosopher Augustine refers to in Book VII (**211-16**). He makes the case that Augustine accepted Plotinus's fallen soul doctrine, at least in his early writings. Van Fleteren, on the other hand, believes that Augustine studied Porphyry as well as Plotinus (**225-28**). He claims that O'Connell over-emphasizes the pessimistic fallen soul doctrine. The mystical ascent of the soul, not its fall, is the central motif of Augustine's early writings, including the *Confessions*, according to Van Fleteren. Van Fleteren's position is informed by the earlier work of his teacher, O'Meara (**217-20**). O'Meara provides excellent brief reviews of the "Platonic books" problem (**217-18**).

Ethics (**185-90**), the nature of human memory (**191-96**), and several other philosophical issues relevant to the *Confessions* have also been investigated by modern scholars.

PSYCHOLOGICAL CRITICISM

American philosopher William James published the first psychological evaluation of the *Confessions* in 1902 (**303**). In his brief remarks, James views Augustine as a perfect example of the "divided self," which is the psychological basis for his famous twice-born character type. While highly regarded and occasionally influential (*see*: **292, 300, 361**), James's work has not been seminal in *Confessions* scholarship because it does not fit within the framework of Freudian analysis, which has been dominant. Freud's influence spawned two competing schools of *Confessions* interpretation: Oedipal and narcissistic.

Charles Kligerman (**281**) points out Augustine's unresolved Oedipal conflicts in his reading of the *Confessions*. He is particularly interested in Augustine's comparison of Aeneas's lover, Dido, to his own mother. In a more recent article, Paul Rigby argues that Augustine was able to resolve his Oedipal conflicts in an appropriate fashion (**282**). As these two interpretations demonstrate, the range of psychological assessment has been wide: Kligerman views Augustine as mentally ill, yet Rigby sees him as well adjusted. In general, the earlier interpretations (prior to a first symposium on the *Confessions* sponsored by the *Journal for the Scientific Study of Religion* in 1965-66) are more clinical and less sympathetic to Augustine. Don Browning's review essay (**279**) provides an excellent evaluation of the Freudian interpretations.

Donald Capps (**286**) outlines what a narcissistic interpretation of the *Confessions* would entail, claiming that Oedipal readings overlook the crucial issue of Augustine's inability to love others. Here we see the competitive contrast between Oedipal and narcissistic schools of Freudian thought. (The link to Freud is less significant for narcissism, but nevertheless real.) True to form, David Bakan's relatively early narcissistic interpretation is harsh (**284**); he accuses Augustine of covering up a perverse power struggle with God.

There have been many attempts to limit or criticize the Freudian influence upon *Confessions* scholarship. Capps (**288**) offers an Allportian analysis of Augustine in an attempt to break free from the Freudian emphasis. Paula Fredriksen (**294**) believes that most psychoanalytic interpretations of Augustine make hasty Freudian generalizations that do not hold up under historical scrutiny. She recommends Peter Brown's study of Augustine (**128**) as a model for writing psychobiography.

Like Fredriksen, other scholars have also explored the problems of psychohistory in the context of *Confessions* scholarship. Paul Archambault believes that psychological insights are, at best, only partially useful to the historian (**291**). He also thinks it is naïve to expect psychoanalytic language to capture the sense of religious experience. Diane Jonte-Pace (**295**) compares twentieth century Augustinian psychohistory to nineteenth century quests for the historical Jesus. She expects the confusion in Augustinian scholarship to be cleared up by another Schweitzer. Eugene TeSelle claims that an historically sensitive and theologically informed interpretation of Augustine would be superior to any Oedipal or narcissistic interpretation (**296**).

Not surprisingly, much psychological attention has been focused upon Augustine's sexuality. What is surprising, however, is that most of the scholarly work pertaining to the *Confessions* has been in defense of Augustine's views. Peter Brown (**306**) and David Hunter (**309**) caution that it was not until later in life that Augustine linked sexuality to sin, which then had a profound and negative (according to modern standards) influence upon Western civilization. In earlier writings such as the *Confessions*, Augustine's views were anything but pessimistic. *See also*: **311-16**.

SPIRITUALITY AND READER GUIDANCE

One way to judge the vigor of an ancient classic such as the *Confessions* is to notice how many articles and books are being written about how to read it and teach it. A sampling of such writings is included in this chapter. Many are not scholarly writings. Robert Allen, for example, tries to explain why the *Confessions* appealed to him in a popular press magazine article (**321**). This is a fascinating aspect of the modern life of Augustine's book, worthy of inclusion in this bibliography. *See also*: **325, 330-33, 336, 339, 343.**

Scholars play their part in the ongoing popular appeal of the *Confessions* by writing critical reading guides (*see*: **326, 328, 337**). Often the purpose in such writings is to reintroduce Western spirituality to a secular culture. Scholars also lecture about Augustine's life and times, then publish their lectures (*see*: **322, 327, 329, 338**). They also make arguments about why the *Confessions* ought to be taught in school (*see*: **369, 372-74**).

A number of articles have been written about mystical (or near-mystical) experiences that Augustine recorded in the *Confessions*. Paul Henry (**359**) links two such experiences (Augustine's first encounter with Neoplatonism at Milan, his conversations with Monica at Ostia) by suggesting that they were two aspects of the same religious quest for God. John Mourant (**363-64**) and Wilma Von Jess (**366**) have debated whether the Ostia experience described in Book IX was truly mystical or not. *See also*: **360-62, 365.**

Somewhat related to the popular spirituality theme of this chapter are studies devoted to Augustine's mother, Monica. Margaret O'Ferrall (**354**) and several others (**351, 355, 357**) try to determine what can be known about Monica given the fact that the *Confessions* is our only source of information. Ferrari investigates the dreams of Monica that are recorded in the *Confessions*, concluding that Augustine viewed them as a manifestation of God's will (**348-50**).

STRUCTURAL UNITY OF THE TEXT

The first nine books of the *Confessions* are autobiographical, telling the story of how Augustine rejected the Catholicism of his childhood, then returned to it in his early thirties. Books X-XIII, on the other hand, are something altogether different. In Book X, Augustine returns to the present time of his writing, twelve years after the last scenes of Book IX, and begins a series of theological meditations. Books XI-XIII continue in the meditative style, but are more focused upon how to understand God's Word, particularly Genesis 1:1. How to explain this puzzling shift in style and purpose is one of the significant questions of modern *Confessions* criticism.

In general, English language scholars have avoided the suggestion that Augustine was a poor writer, passing off two different books as one. Instead, they have offered a variety of suggestions for how to view the text as a unified whole. For example, Robert Crouse (**377**) argues that the three parts of the text (books I-IX, X, XI-XIII) correspond to three stages of mystical ascent (from *exterioria* to *interioria* to *superioria*). Similarly, Colin Starnes (**380**) suggests that the three parts correspond to the three persons of the trinity; N. Joseph Torchia (**383**) that the parts correspond to vices of pride, curiosity, and carnal concupiscence; and Ralph Flores (**387**) that the parts are structured according to activities of writing, speaking, and exegesis. *See also*: **384, 401-09, 413.**

Other scholars have argued that the unity problem is a consequence of modern misreadings of the *Confessions*. Gerald Bonner (**385**) claims that we are confused by the three part structure because we want to read the *Confessions* as a simple psychological autobiography, which it is not. Marjorie O'Rourke Boyle (**399**) emphasizes the rhetorical nature of Augustine's text, which follows a pattern that modern readers no longer understand. *See also*: **415**.

Another explanatory tactic is to focus upon one book of the *Confessions* as most crucial, and therefore unifying for the whole. Thomas Callaghan (**390**), Emmet Flood (**392**), and James O'Donnell (**394**) view Book X as the central turning point. According to Callaghan, Augustine's mention of Christ in Book X signals a shift from restless searching to peaceful meditation, which accounts for the shift in compositional style. *See also*: **391, 393, 395-96**.

Yet another tactic is to highlight symbolic or thematic imagery that serves as a structuring principle for the text. Marjorie Suchocki (**382**) argues that the *Confessions* is structured around the appearance of two trees (the pear tree in Book II, the fig tree in Book VIII) which correspond to the two trees in the garden of Eden (the tree of the knowledge of good and evil, the tree of life). *See also*: **378-79, 386, 397, 411, 413, 416, 418, 420**.

THEOLOGICAL INTERPRETATION

The earliest modern scholars such as Harnack (**170**) certainly understood the *Confessions* as a theological text. But they did not investigate the nature of theology in their criticism of Augustine's classic. That is a relatively recent development. In 1961, Kenneth Burke published an unusual book (**430**) in which he compared theology (words about God) to logology (words about words). Relying upon the *Confessions*, Burke shed light upon the nature of theology by viewing it as a model rhetorical system. David Burrell claims that we learn how theology is grounded in lived experience when we read the *Confessions* (**431**). George Stroup (**438**) and Sallie McFague TeSelle (**439**) extend Burrell's insight further, suggesting that the personal theology of the *Confessions* can help remake contemporary theology, which is in a state of crisis. On the other hand, Joseph O'Leary (**436**) and Mark Taylor (**124**) read the *Confessions* as the source of an irrelevant, harmful metaphysical theology. *See also*: **432-35, 437, 440**.

A number of studies have investigated how the *Confessions* contributes to debates about theological issues, particularly God, sin, and scripture. O'Connell explores images of God (wind and nurse, for example) found in the *Confessions* (**426**); Ritamary Bradley, on the other hand, studies how Augustine was able to conflate biblical and Neoplatonic notions of the divine (**425**). Ferrari (**446**) and William Mann (**447**) try to understand why Augustine makes such a big deal about stealing pears as a youth; it seems such a forgivable, little sin. Mann (**448**) and Gareth Matthews (**449**) explore the case of "wet dreams" that Augustine mentions in Book X when he suggests that it is possible to sin while sleeping. Several scholars have explored Augustine's use of psalms in the *Confessions* (**456, 465-66**). Ferrari, a prolific *Confessions* scholar, has made extensive studies of Augustine's use of scripture (**457-62**). *See also*: **427-29, 445, 450-55, 463-64, 467-68**.

Finally, there are a few studies that pertain to Augustine's search for truth. Raymond DiLorenzo, for example, argues that Augustine invented a new style of philosophizing in the *Confessions* which links truth to piety rather than reason (**442**). Margaret Miles tries to rehabilitate Augustine's theory of illumination, which requires human effort in order to see the truth (**444**). Brook Manville suggests that Augustine's self-examination, recorded in the *Confessions*, was a response to the Donatists who insisted that bishops must be perfect in order to be true bishops (**423**).

2

Autobiographical Studies

COMPARATIVE ANALYSIS

See also: 027, 061, 065, 091, 105, 238

001   Archambault, Paul. "Rousseau's Tactical (Mis)reading of Augustine." *Symposium: A Quarterly Journal in Modern Foreign Literatures* 41 (Spring 1987): 6-14.

Why did Rousseau claim that his *Confessions* was without precedent? According to Archambault, his neglect of Augustine's autobiography was a veiled refutation of Catholic anthropology. He suggests that we read the two works as one text: two voices in animated, often hostile conversation.

002   Boyle, Marjorie O'Rourke. "A Likely Story: The Autobiographical as Epideictic." *Journal of the American Academy of Religion* 57 (Spring 1989): 23-51.

Boyle focuses upon four famous conversion sites (Augustine's garden, Petrach's mountain, Cusanus's sea, and Luther's tower) in order to demonstrate a common misunderstanding of epideictic rhetorical texts as spiritual autobiographies. Epideictic rhetoric has a moral purpose whereas autobiography has an historical and psychological purpose. *See also*: **399**.

003   Brumble, H. David. "Sam Blowsnake's Confessions: *Crashing Thunder* and the History of American Indian Autobiography." *Canadian Review of American Studies* 16 (Fall 1985): 271-82.

Relying upon Weintraub's work (**045**), Brumble thinks American Indian autobiography recapitulates the history of Euro-American autobiography. He argues that Sam Blowsnake's *Crashing Thunder* is the first genuine Indian autobiography, comparable to Augustine's *Confessions*. Like Augustine, Blowsnake overcomes his misguided ways through creative synthesis of traditional Winnebago culture and the Peyote Cult (much as Augustine overcame his misguided ways through synthesis of Neoplatonism and Christianity).

004   Chivers, Frances. "Wordsworth's *Prelude* in the Tradition of Augustine's *Confessions.*" *Augustinian Studies* 13 (1982): 31-42.

Chivers wants to demonstrate that Wordsworth represents a modern expression of the religious and literary tradition that stems from Augustine. He claims that similarities between the *Prelude* and the *Confessions* are a consequence of Wordsworth's and Augustine's similar religious and introspective natures.

005   Conely, James. "Petrarch and Augustine: The *Canzoniere* and the *Confessions.*" *Augustinian Studies* 14 (1983): 35-44.

Conely believes that Petrarch and Augustine shared similar notions of the world, friends, and God, and it is on that basis that Petrarch's 364 poems can be said to imitate the *Confessions*.

006   De Mijolla, Elizabeth. *Autobiographical Quests: Augustine, Montaigne, Rousseau, and Wordsworth.* Charlottesville, VA: University Press of Virginia, 1994.

De Mijolla interprets autobiographical writing in terms of tension between mimesis and memory. Mimesis is the traditional pole, where order, history, and communication dominate; memory is the individual pole, disorderly, achronological and afigural. Mimesis dominates in the early life of the genre, as Augustine's *Confessions* demonstrate; as time passes, the trend is toward the disorderly.

007   Dombrowski, Daniel. "The *Confessions* of St. Augustine and De Quincey." *Augustinian Studies* 18 (1987): 151-64.

Dombrowski compares Augustine's *Confessions* and De Quincey's *Confessions of an English Opium Eater*. He argues that De Quincey can be better understood through a consideration of the *Confessions*, and that Augustine can be made more intelligible to modern persons through comparison with De Quincey's romantic counterpart.

008   Harper, Ralph. "Remembering Eternity: St. Augustine and Proust." *Thought: A Review of Culture and Idea* 34 (Winter 1959): 569-606.

Harper compares the disquietude that led Augustine to God with the regret that led Proust to himself. He contrasts their different ways to recovery, which entail different understandings of memory. Finally, Harper criticises Proust for lacking theological depth.

009 Hawkins, Anne. *Archetypes of Conversion: The Spiritual Autobiographies of St. Augustine, John Bunyan, and Thomas Merton.* Lewisburg, PA: Bucknell University Press, 1985.

Hawkins discusses archetypal patterns found in spiritual autobiographies from every phase or period of Christian history: pilgrimage, *psychomachia* (battle between good and evil forces for the soul), familial characterization, and conversion. She types the three autobiographies under investigation according to their conversions: Augustine's follows a crisis or heroic paradigm, Bunyan's a conflictive one, Merton's sacramental. Hawkins indicates why the distinction between secular and spiritual autobiography is important; the latter is concerned with the soul's relation to God, not just the self.

010 Hopkins, Brooke. "Pear-Stealing and Other Faults: An Essay on Confessional Autobiography." *South Atlantic Quarterly* 80 (1981): 305-21.

Hopkins demonstrates how confession of theft figures prominently in the construction and meaning of three autobiographies: Augustine's *Confessions* (theft of pears), Rousseau's *Confessions* (theft of ribbon), and Wordsworth's *Prelude* (theft of boat).

011 Hopkins, Brooke. "Reading, and Believing, in Autobiography." *Soundings: An Interdisciplinary Journal* 64 (Spring 1981): 93-111.

Hopkins investigates three autobiographers (Augustine, Rousseau, Wordsworth), asking how they overcame the paradox of making public their private selves. He claims that autobiographers require an audience of believers or sympathetic readers in order to make their self-revelations truthful. Each of the three appealed to a slightly different human experience of shared sympathy: Augustine to the holy spirit, Rousseau to conscience, and Wordsworth to memory.

012 Irlam, Shaun. "Showing Losses, Counting Gains: 'Scenes' from Negative Autobiography." *MLN* 106 (December 1991): 997-1009.

Irlam discerns two parallel models of memory and autobiography in Book X of the *Confessions*. The positive model is obvious: memory is a rich storehouse from which one recollects experience in order to construct a self-narrative. Less obvious is the negative model of forgetting which also provides a kind of negative self-knowledge. Irlam verifies this reading of Book X by referring to other famous autobiographies.

013 Koretz, Gene. "Augustine's *Confessions* and the *Education* of Henry Adams." *Comparative Literature* 12 (1960): 193-206.

Koretz explores how Adams used the *Confessions* as a model for his *Education*. Adams especially admired Augustine's combination of narrative and didactic styles. Koretz compares the two autobiographies, demonstrating Adams's debt to Augustine.

014   Kuntz, Paul. "Linear or Cyclical Order? Contrasting Confessions of Augustine, Vico, and Joyce." *Soundings: An Interdisciplinary Journal* 75 (Winter 1992): 517-36.

Kuntz interprets Vico's *Autobiography* and Joyce's *Portrait* in terms of Augustine's *Confessions*. He contrasts their efforts to fuse together linear and cyclical (biblical and Greek) understandings of historical time.

015   Lifson, Martha. "Creation and the Self in *Paradise Lost* and the *Confessions*." *Centennial Review* 19 (1975): 187-97.

Lifson compares Augustine's and Milton's use of chaos imagery to depict their fallen states, and their use of creation imagery to depict salvation or recovery from chaos.

016   Lionnet-McCumber, Francoise. *Autobiographical Tongues: (Self-) Reading and (Self-)Writing in Augustine, Nietzsche, Maya Angelou, Marie Cardinal, and Marie-Therese Humbert.* Ph.D. dissertation, University of Michigan, 1986.

Lionnet-McCumber analyzes the linguistic mechanisms by which autobiographers become self-dissimulating in order to accomodate more than one cultural tradition. She regards the apparent incoherence of the *Confessions* as such a mechanism.

017   O'Meara, John. "The *Confession* of St. Patrick and the *Confessions* of St. Augustine." *Irish Ecclesiastical Record* 85 (March 1956): 190-97.

O'Meara investigates Patrick's possible use of the *Confessions* in writing his own *Confession*. He concludes that there are no sure echoes of Augustine in Patrick; the Bible is more clearly the inspiration for Patrick's *Confession*.

018   Paolini, Shirley. *Confessions of Sin and Love in the Middle Ages: Dante's Commedia and St. Augustine's Confessions.* Washington: University Press of America, 1982.

Based on a Ph.D. dissertation, University of California. Paolini examines the Christian and classical sources of Augustine's confessional autobiography. She finds traces of ritualistic formulas that link the *Confessions* to Dante's later *Commedia*, which she interprets as a more advanced expression of the genre Augustine invented.

019 Penaskovic, Richard. "Saint Augustine's *Confessions* and Newman's *Apologia*: Similarities and Differences." *Augustinian Studies* 9 (1978): 81-91.

Penaskovic compares the autobiographies of Augustine and Newman on their use of scripture, attitude toward friends, creative expression, and common search for truth.

020 Thompson, Caleb. *Wittgenstein's Confessions: A Study of the Influence of Augustine's and Tolstoy's Confessions on the Philosophy of Wittgenstein.* Ph.D. dissertation, University of Virginia, 1994.

Thompson believes that Wittgenstein's writings belong to the forgotten genre of philosophical confession, which he demonstrates through comparative readings with Augustine *Confessions* (*Philosophical Investigations*) and Tolstoy's *Confessions* (*Tractatus*).

021 Van Horne, Winston. "From Sinners to Saints: The *Confessions* of Saint Augustine and Malcolm X." *Journal of Religious Thought* 43 (Spring-Summer 1986): 76-101.

Four themes (rebellion, revelation, redemption, and regeneration) unite Augustine's *Confessions* and Malcolm X's *Autobiography* according to Van Horne's comparative reading.

022 Warner, Martin. "Philosophical Autobiography: St. Augustine and John Stuart Mill." In *Philosophy and Literature*, ed. by A. Griffiths, 189-210. New York: Cambridge University Press, 1984.

Philosophy usually leads to questions about one's humanity and its place in nature. Unfortunately, it is difficult to confirm and refute answers to such questions. Warner looks at two autobiographies in order to test a contextual, cumulative case method of philosophical assessment. He finds Augustine's theory of humanity in the *Confessions* plausible, but not probative.

023 Zebrak, Michael. *Metanoia and Apostasy: The Journey of the Self in the Confessions of Augustine and the Canzoniere of Petrarch.* Ph.D. dissertation, Rutgers University, 1994.

Zebrak contrasts the post-conversion unity achieved by the narrator of the *Confessions* to the post-conversion fragmentation portrayed in the *Canzoniere*. Petrarch's presentation of life as a series of struggles without eschatological climax is more realistic according to Zebrak.

GENRE THEORY

See also: **002, 006, 038, 041, 052, 067, 069-70, 279, 337, 385, 388, 389**

024   Archambault, Paul. "Augustine, Memory, and the Development of Autobiography." *Augustinian Studies* 13 (1982): 23-30.

Archambault explains why Augustine felt compelled to write Book X of the *Confessions*, specifically how the inquiry into the nature of memory contributes to the autobiography. He argues that Augustine's discussion of memory was necessitated by a change in his understanding of language: from thinking that humans create language to realizing that they are its instrument. That the later books of the *Confessions* are less personal and "autobiographical" is the result of a typically Christian progression away from undue self-regard.

025   Archambault, Paul. "Augustine, Time, and Autobiography as Language." *Augustinian Studies* 15 (1984): 7-14.

Archambault investigates Augustine's parallel understanding of time and language in Book XI of the *Confessions*. Both phenomena are imperfect derivations from divine attributes of Eternity and Word. Writing his autobiography, Augustine transcribed the intimations of his prior belonging to a more perfect realm in his temporal, linguistic existence.

026   Dilthey, Wilhelm. *Pattern and Meaning in History: Thoughts on History and Society.* Edited and introduced by H. Rickman. New York: Harper and Row, 1961.

Dilthey, the great philosopher and historian, claims that autobiography is the most instructive literary-historical category for understanding life. He interprets the *Confessions*, briefly, as one of several direct expressions of reflection on life. In writing the *History of Autobiography*, Georg Misch followed through on Dilthey's insight about the importance of autobiography (**052**).

027   Egan, Susanna. *Patterns of Experience in Autobiography.* Chapel Hill, NC: University of North Carolina Press, 1984.

Egan identifies four common narrative patterns in autobiographical writing: paradise, journey, conversion, and confession. She claims that these patterns persist because they fulfill a mythic and psychological need of self-understanding. She interprets the *Confessions* in the chapter on confession, along with Petrarch's *Secret* and Bunyan's *Grace Abounding*.

028   Frye, Northrop. *Anatomy of Criticism: Four Essays.* Princeton, NJ: Princeton University Press, 1957.

In the fourth essay of this classic, "Rhetorical Criticism: Theory of Genre's," Frye briefly discusses autobiography (or confession) as a form related to the fictional novel. He mentions Augustine as the apparent inventor of confessional prose.

029 Gunn, Janet. *Autobiography: Toward a Poetics of Experience.*
Philadelphia: University of Pennsylvania Press, 1982.

Autobiographical theory has neglected the *bios* or life aspect of auto-bios-graphy according to Gunn. She corrects the problem by attending to the worldly, cultural nature of autobiographical writing. Every autobiographer is first of all a reader of life experience which inspires the act of literary expression. In her reading of the *Confessions*, Gunn demonstrates that Augustine's *credo ut intelligam* is the worldly context for any autobiographical act.

030 Harpham, Geoffrey. "Conversion and the Language of Autobiography."
In *Studies in Autobiography*, ed. by James Olney, 42-50. New Haven, CT: Yale University Press, 1986.

Harpham argues that autobiography is the conversion of life into literature or language. He links this general interpretation of autobiography to Augustine's *Confessions*, demonstrating how the recording of his conversion is artful imitation of other textually "converted" lives. He takes issue with Vance's claim (**388**) that Augustine's conversion signals a divine transgression of his life's story.

031 Howarth, William. "Some Principles of Autobiography." *New Literary History: A Journal of Theory and Interpretation* 5 (Winter 1974): 363-81.

Claiming that autobiography is self-portraiture, Howarth looks to painting in order to identify three distinct autobiographical strategies (oratory, drama, poetry). He claims that the *Confessions* is the best example of an oratorical strategy. His chief concern is to establish the unique sophistication of autobiographical literature.

032 Pascal, Roy. *Design and Truth in Autobiography.* Cambridge, MA: Harvard University Press, 1960.

Pascal claims that every autobiography is essentially an account of the truth of a life. He develops this understanding of the genre by delineating a variety of forms that such truth seeking takes. Augustine's *Confessions*, he says, is of the "acquisition of an outlook" type.

033 Spengemann, William. *The Forms of Autobiography: Episodes in the History of a Literary Genre.* New Haven, CT: Yale University Press, 1980.

Spengemann interprets the history of Western autobiography as a movement from biographical to fictional accounts of selfhood. Augustine's *Confessions* stands at the beginning of this history, and foreshadows its historical, philosophical, and poetic stages. Includes an extensive bibliographic essay on the study of autobiography.

034   Steinhauser, Kenneth. "Augustine's Autobiographical Covenant: A Contemporary Reading of his *Confessions.*" *Perspectives in Religious Studies* 18 (Fall 1991): 233-40.

Steinhauser defines the autobiographical act as the art of self-invention, and the role of the reader as guarantor of the autobiographer's truthfulness (or covenant). Then he turns to Augustine's *Confessions* in order to flesh out his theory of autobiography.

NATURE OF THE SELF

See also: **015-16, 033-34, 058, 060, 071, 104**

035   Babcock, William. "Patterns of Roman Selfhood: Marcus Aurelius and Augustine of Hippo." *Perkins Journal* 29 (Winter 1976): 1-19.

The Roman empire did not support a private literature that reveals the individual person. Two remarkable exceptions, according to Babcock, are the *Meditations* of Marcus Aurelius and the *Confessions* of Augustine. Both men (one prior to Constantine's epochal conversion, one after) were converted to philosophy from rhetoric, which, according to Babcock, was the basis for their uncharacteristically personal writings. Both wrestled with alienation; Babcock believes that Augustine's solution was better.

036   Brownlee, Marina. "Autobiography as Self-(re)presentation: The Augustinian Paradigm and Juan Ruiz's Theory of Reading." In *Mimesis: From Mirror to Method, Augustine to Descartes*, ed. by John Lyons and S. Nichols, 71-82. Hanover, NH: University Press of New England, 1982.

Brownlee interprets Ruiz's enigmatic *Book of Good Love* as a sceptical, nonexemplary rewriting of Augustine's *Confessions*. Ruiz is more appreciative of human foibles than Augustine, which limit the value of imitative texts. Reading is each reader's particular problem for Ruiz, whereas Augustine expected his book to stand as an impetus to conversion for every reader.

037   Elbaz, Robert. *The Changing Nature of the Self: A Critical Study of the Autobiographic Discourse.* Iowa City, IA: University of Iowa Press, 1987.

Elbaz investigates the negative consequences of self-ownership as presented in modern autobiographies. In a preliminary chapter on the *Confessions*, he emphasizes the parallels between small facts and metaphysical interpretation, thereby accounting for the unity of the text. He also emphasizes the mixture of classical and biblical styles.

038   Freccero, John. "Autobiography and Narrative." In *Reconstructing Individualism: Autonomy, Individuality, and the Self in Western Thought*, ed. by

Thomas Heller, Morton Sosna, and David Wellbery, 16-29. Stanford, CA: Stanford University Press, 1986.

Freccero reads the *Confessions* according to the Nietzschean insight that individuality is achieved only by its own destruction. Autobiography as genre implies the death of self as character and the resurrection of self as author. In Augustine's case, the sinner is killed for the sake of the saint. Freccero's claim is that individualism is inconceivable without literary expression.

039   Gusdorf, Georges. "Conditions and Limits of Autobiography." In *Autobiography: Essays Theoretical and Critical*, ed. and trans. by James Olney, 28-48. Princeton, NJ: Princeton University Press, 1980.

Gusdorf explores the cultural and philosophical presuppositions of autobiography understood as a self-conscious stance toward one's own personality. To be an historian of personal destiny is ultimately an artistic work of mythic proportions according to Gusdorf.

040   Hartle, Ann. *The Modern Self in Rousseau's Confessions: A Reply to St. Augustine*. Revisions: A Series of Books on Ethics. Notre Dame, IN: University of Notre Dame Press, 1983.

Since the publication of Rousseau's *Confessions*, we have taken for granted the notion of an "inner self." Hartle analyzes Rousseau's choices (which include rejecting Augustine and Plutarch) in the constitution of modern self-identity. Rousseau's portrait of himself returning to an uncorrupted state of nature is the modern secular equivalent of Augustine's earlier portrait of himself returning to God.

041   Jay, Paul. *The Recollected Self: Figuration and Transformation in Creative Autobiography*. Santa Cruz, CA: University of California, 1981.

Ph.D. dissertation. Jay investigates how autobiographers find a way to extend past experiences into present literary activity through creative textual strategies. He discusses Augustine's *Confessions*, as well as the autobiographies of Wordsworth, Joyce, Proust, Eliot, and Barthes.

042   Lloyd, Genevieve. "The Self as Fiction: Philosophy and Autobiography." *Philosophy and Literature* 10 (October 1986): 168-85.

Lloyd contrasts the autobiographical reflections of Augustine, Rousseau, and Sartre on themes of temporality, selfhood, and truth. She is primarily concerned with how Augustine and Rousseau attempt to grasp the true nature of the self (reconciling subjective and objective perspectives), and Sartre's view that such an effort is illusory.

043   Lyons, John. *The Invention of the Self: The Hinge of Consciousness in the Eighteenth Century.* Carbondale, IL: Southern Illinois University Press, 1978.

Lyons investigates the rise of self-consciousness in its modern form. In a chapter on autobiography, he contrasts Augustine's *Confessions* with autobiographical writings from different decades in the eighteenth century.

044   Olsen, Glenn. "St. Augustine and the Problem of the Medieval Discovery of the Individual." *Word and Spirit: A Monastic Review* 9 (1987): 129-56.

Olsen argues that medieval people (Abelard, for example) often had an Augustinian sense of the developing self, which implies that individualism is not the exclusive possession of modern people as Weintraub (**045**) and others claim.

045   Weintraub, Karl. *The Value of the Individual: Self and Circumstance in Autobiography.* Chicago: University of Chicago Press, 1978.

Weintraub writes an historical essay on the gradual emergence of individuality in autobiographical writings from Augustine to Goethe. Interpreting the *Confessions*, he tries to understand how Augustine understood himself, that is, as a typical pilgrim rather than as a unique individual. Much of what is wrong with modernity, the bad or excessive individualism, must be traced to Rousseau, not Augustine (and Goethe), according to Weintraub.

PERIOD STUDIES

See also: **004-05, 007-09, 011, 018, 023, 026, 033, 035, 043-45, 064, 081, 084, 091, 099**

046   Danahay, Martin. *A Community of One: Masculine Autobiography and Autonomy in Nineteenth-Century Britain.* The Margins of Literature. Albany, NY: State University of New York Press, 1993.

Danahay claims that the *Confessions* is not an autobiography because Augustine (1) makes no claims to originality or uniqueness, and (2) predates the eighteenth-century invention of copyright. Augustine's text aims to create readers in its own image; its ideal is imitation. The *Confessions* is thoroughly communal, which means that it borrows from and dialogues with many other texts.

047   Dunne, John. *A Search for God in Time and Memory.* Notre Dame, IN: University of Notre Dame Press, 1977.

Dunne investigates personal life stories from ancient to modern times, thereby developing a framework for understanding how modern people differ from ancient people, and how they might benefit from sympathetic "passing over" to an ancient perspective. He claims that the *Confessions* is the archetypal autobiography because Augustine conceived life as a story of personal experience. He uses Augustine's story to introduce the important ancient concept of recollection.

048 Fleishman, Avrom. *Figures of Autobiography: The Language of Self-Writing in Victorian and Modern England.* Berkeley, CA: University of California Press, 1983.

Rather than investigate the indeterminate nature of autobiography as a literary genre, Fleishman looks at self-writing activities from one historical period. First, however, he interprets the *Confessions*, arguing that the originality of Augustine's text lies in its mythic qualities, that is, its ability to order disparate materials into significant form. The rhetorical possibilities of autobiographical figuration are established in Augustine's Christian mythology.

049 Gillespie, Dennis. *Augustine and America: Five Contemporary Autobiographical Works.* Chicago: Loyola University, 1988.

Ph.D. dissertation. Gillespie reads five contemporary autobiographers (Merrill, Ashbery, Bidart, Hejinian, Lowell) in light of Augustine's *Confessions*. He claims that Augustine's autobiography anticipates modern preoccupation with life's fragmentation and uncertainty. The difference is that modern autobiographers no longer find comfort in Augustine's faith.

050 Hilary, Christine. *The Confessio Tradition from Augustine to Chaucer.* Berkeley, CA: University of California, 1979.

Ph.D. dissertation. Hilary explores the shared world of religious and secular confessions in the Middle Ages, which she calls the literary *confessio* tradition. It includes such disparate confessors as Augustine and the Wife of Bath.

051 Kijowski, Andrzej. "*Postscripta* to Saint Augustine's *Confessions.*" In *Four Decades of Polish Essays*, ed. by J. Kott, 195-216. Evanston, IL: NorthWestern University Press, 1990.

This is a subtle discussion of the similarities and differences between modern times and Augustine's times. Kijowski upholds the Augustinian insight that the soul cannot live without the joy of God found in faith. He contrasts contemporary autobiographies (often joyless preludes to suicide) with Augustine's ode to faith.

052 Misch, Georg. *A History of Autobiography in Antiquity.* 2 vols. Trans. by E. Dickes. Cambridge, MA: Harvard University Press, 1951.

Dilthey's son-in-law and intellectual heir (**026**), Misch is the master historian of autobiography. In a chapter on the *Confessions*, he contrasts that text with

Augustine's earlier *Soliliquies*; makes clear what is unique (and not unique) about Augustine's autobiography relative to other writings from the classical world; and discusses the structure of Augustine's autobiography.

053   Renna, Thomas. "Augustinian Autobiography: Medieval and Modern." *Augustinian Studies* 11 (1980): 197-203.

Renna believes that spiritual autobiographies in the west reflect their times more than is recognized. In the Middle Ages, for example, monks wrote autobiographies in an effort to reform ascetic practice. Nevertheless, the trend from Augustine to Merton has been to compress ascetic traditions into the single aspect of contemplation.

054   Tsanoff, Radoslav. *Autobiographies of Ten Religious Leaders: Alternatives in Christian Experience.* San Antonio, TX: Trinity University Press, 1968.

Tsanoff's book is a biographical introduction to the humanities, or, in this case, the varieties of Christian experience. He presents the *Confessions* as essential for study of the formation and exposition of Christian beliefs.

055   West, Andrew. *Roman Autobiography, Particularly Augustine's Confessions.* New York: De Vinne Press, 1901.

In this lecture, West reviews the history of ancient Latin autobiography. He focuses upon Augustine's *Confessions*, calling it the first introspective autobiography. West is one of the first English language interpreters to mention Harnack's problematic views (**173**). The lecture ends with a brief comparison of modern autogiobraphies to the *Confessions*.

RELIGIOSITY

See also: **009, 049, 051, 053-54, 093, 117, 119**

056   Barbour, John. *The Conscience of the Autobiographer: Ethical and Religious Dimensions of Autobiography.* Studies in Literature and Religion. London: Macmillan, 1992.

Barbour interprets classic autobiographies as ethical (and, in some cases, religious) documents of conscience understood as moral self-assessment. In a chapter on "Conscience and Truthfulness," he uses the *Confessions* to demonstrate the working of conscience in autobiographical writing. Conscience is an important incentive for autobiography, according to Barbour. It also monitors autobiography, and sponsors an ideal to correct self-deception.

057   Barbour, John. *Versions of Deconversion: Autobiography and the Loss of*

Faith. Charlottesville, VA: University Press of Virginia, 1994.

Interested in the reasons (usually ethical) for rejecting religious faith, as well as the way such stories are told, Barbour analyzes autobiographies that document losses of faith (deconversion narratives). He begins with the *Confessions*, focusing upon Augustine's ten year struggle to break away from Manicheism.

058 Byrne, Lawrence. "Writing God's Story: Self and Narrative Structure in Augustine's *Confessions*." *Christianity and Literature* 38 (1989): 15-31.

Byrne investigates the special problems of religious autobiographical writing, particularly the need to defer to God as ultimate author of the self's remaking itself. Variations in the structure of the *Confessions*, particularly the turn to scripture in the later books, are a consequence of changes in Augustine's narratival struggles to overcome himself. See also **116**.

059 Capps, Donald. "Parabolic Events in Augustine's Autobiography." *Theology Today* 40 (October 1983): 260-72.

Capps uses the *Confessions* to demonstrate how autobiography illuminates the self like parable reveals God. Parabolic events are life occasions where the occasion becomes a metaphor for one's whole life. Capps focuses upon three such unusually disclosive events in Augustine's life (the pear-stealing episode, the death of his friend, and the conversion experience in the garden). He argues that Augustine's habit of self-reproach is the result of shame, not guilt.

060 Evans, James. "Prisoner of the Flesh: A Literary Analysis of Augustine's *Confessions*." *AME Zion Quarterly Review* (January 1987): 14-22.

Evans examines three images from the *Confessions* which have become tropes for the genre of spiritual autobiography: self-discovery in the garden, personal conversion, and the relation between the regenerate self and the unconverted self. Evans points out that Augustine's association of sin with blackness, stain, and flesh or sexuality has had a negative cultural influence.

061 Gilpatrick, Naomi. "Autobiographies of Grace." *Catholic World* 159 (April 1944): 52-7.

Gilpatrick reads Augustine's *Confessions* and Bunyan's *Grace Abounding* as stories of friendship and striving for grace.

062 Gunn, Janet. "The Religious Hermeneutic of Autobiography: Augustine's *Confessions* and the *Credo ut Intelligam*." In *Art/Literature/Religion: Life on the Borders*, ed. by Robert Detweiler, 61-70. *Journal of the American Academy of Religion Thematic Studies*, 49/2. Chico, CA: Scholars Press, 1983.

Gunn reads the *Confessions* from the point of view of the "autobiographical situation," which entails three moments of interpretive significance (impulse, perspective, response). She reevaluates the autobiographical status of the *Confessions*, and determines that *credo ut intelligam* (believe in order to understand) constitutes the religious significance of Augustine's text.

063   Hamilton, Andrew. "The *Confessions*: Autobiographical Theology." *Colloquium* 17 (October 1984): 33-42.

Hamilton attempts to overcome modern difficulties with the *Confessions* (puzzlement over Augustine's harsh recollection of his sins, the structural unity of the text, etc.) by claiming it is an apologetic work in autobiographical form. Following O'Connell (**417**), he argues that the purpose of the *Confessions* is to articulate a Christian theodicy that contradicts Manicheism.

064   Kliever, Lonnie. "Confessions of Unbelief: In Quest of the Vital Lie." *Journal for the Scientific Study of Religion* 25 (March 1986): 102-15.

Kliever presents his own spiritual journey as an illustration of our culture's religious evolution. He looks to Augustine's *Confessions* to confirm his claim that autobiography and history come together in stories of religious struggle. Kliever's contrast of traditional and modern religious experience (the former is mythic and truthful, the latter autobiographic and fictional) is creative yet general.

065   Pelikan, Jaraslov. "Writing as a Means of Grace." In *Spiritual Quests: The Art and Craft of Religious Writing*, ed. by William Zinsser, 83-101. Boston: Houghton Mifflin, 1988.

Originally part of a series of talks given at The New York Public Library on behalf of the Book-of-the-Month Club. Pelikan discusses the confessional writings of Augustine, Boethius, and Newman. About the *Confessions*, Pelikan says that Augustine's inward look at his own soul was also an outward look, indirectly, at the face of God.

066   Rothfield, Lawrence. "Autobiography and Perspective in the *Confessions* of St. Augustine." *Comparative Literature* 33 (Summer 1981): 209-23.

Resisting a trend started by Misch (**052**) and Courcelle (**156**), Rothfield attempts to reintroduce theology back into autobiographical studies of the *Confessions*. He claims that Augustine's understanding of Christian incarnation enabled him to see the structural problem of his autobiography as identical to the epistemological problem of his spiritual rebirth.

067   Scott, Jamie. "From Literal Self-Sacrifice to Literary Self-Sacrifice: Augustine's *Confessions* and the Rhetoric of Testimony." In *Augustine: From*

Rhetor to Theologian, ed. by Joanne McWilliam, 31-49. Waterloo, ON: Wilfrid Laurier University Press, 1992.

What type of literature is the *Confessions*? Scott explores this genre question, beginning with criticism of Frye's too simple equation of confessional and autobiographical writing (**028**). Scott argues that it is the structure of testimony (the desire to bear witness to God) that makes Augustine's autobiography distinctively confessional.

068 Stewart, Mary. *The Procession of the Time-Bearing Gods: Soul-History in Autobiography*. Syracuse, NY: Syracuse University, 1982.

Ph.D. dissertation. Stewart argues that autobiographical discourse in its religious dimension is soul-history, meaning that it creates a world in which writer and reader imaginatively understand the pilgrimage of life. She views Augustine's *Confessions* as archetypal in this regard.

069 Troxel, A. Craig. "What did Augustine 'Confess' in His *Confessions*?" *Trinity Journal* 15 (Fall 1994): 163-79.

Troxel claims that the *Confessions* defies genre categories such as autobiography. Nevertheless, the *Confessions* can be properly understood by attending to Augustine's purpose, which was to tell his life story for the glory of God.

070 Vance, Eugene. "The Functions and Limits of Autobiography in Augustine's *Confessions*." *Poetics Today: International Journal for Theory and Analysis of Literature and Communication* 5 (1984): 399-409.

Vance reads the *Confessions* as part of other discourses which, taken together, establish a point of view that ultimately derives from the authority of God's Word. He focuses upon Augustine's problems with fatherhood (first raised in the *Confessions* then resolved in *de trinitate*).

071 Wojciehowski, Dolora. *The Ransoming of Will in the Rhetoric of Confession*. New Haven, CT: Yale University, 1984.

Ph.D. dissertation. Wojciehowski analyzes five medieval autobiographies, beginning with Augustine's *Confessions*, in order to demonstrate the illicit theological use of the will in confessional persuasion. She claims that defense of a transcendent self relies upon defense of the will even though loss of will is purportedly part of the spiritual (transcendent) journey.

3

Classical and Literary Scholarship

AUGUSTINE'S LATIN

See also: **369**

072 Arts, Mary. *The Syntax of the Confessions of Saint Augustine.* Patristic Studies, 14. Washington: Catholic University of America, 1927.

Ph.D. dissertation. Arts studies Augustine's syntax, meaning his peculiar use of nouns, verbs, and so forth. Her conclusion is that Augustine conformed to classical Latin requirements more than any other writer of his times.

073 Caldwell, Ellen. "The *loquaces muti* and the *Verbum infans*: Paradox and Language in the *Confessiones* of St. Augustine." In *Collectanea Augustiniana: Augustine, Second Founder of the Faith*, ed. by Joseph Schnaubelt and Frederick Van Fleteren, 101-11. New York: Peter Lang, 1990.

Caldwell reads the *Confessions* as a verbal act concerned with the inadequacies of speech. This paradox is encoded in all aspects of Augustine's rhetoric, which is never simple, unadorned, or uncalculated.

074 Carroll, M. Borromeo. *The Clausulae in the Confessions of St. Augustine.* Patristic Studies, 62. Washington: The Catholic University of America Press, 1940.

Ph.D. dissertation. Carroll examines the 3,637 clausulae (final clause endings) of the *Confessions* from both metrical and accentual points of view. She makes statistical comparisons, concluding that the *Confessions* is slightly more metrical than ametrical; that its prose differs from other writings by Augustine; and that it is unique among Latin literature of the times.

075 Hrdlicka, Clement. *A Study of the Late Latin Vocabulary and of the Prepositions and the Demonstrative Pronouns in the Confessions of St.*

Augustine. Patristic Studies, 31. Washington: Catholic University of America, 1931.

Ph.D. dissertation. On the basis of his word study of the *Confessions*, Hrdlicka concludes that Augustine's style was a blend of classical, colloquial, rhetorical, and scriptural elements in the Latin of his day. The greatest influences on his vocabulary were Cicero, Virgil, Apuleius, and the scriptures.

CONFESSIONS SCHOLARSHIP

See also: **082, 153, 166-67, 169-70, 173, 215, 218, 279, 289, 294-95, 326, 417**

076   Gorman, Michael. "The Early Manuscript Tradition of St. Augustine's *Confessions*." *Journal of Theological Studies* 34 (April 1983): 114-45.

Gorman discusses the publication history of the *Confessions* and suggests one correction for the critical Skutella edition. Scholarly attention has been concentrated on ninth century manuscripts because only one manuscript of the *Confessions* predates 800.

077   Sillem, Edward. "The *Confessions* of St. Augustine: Review of Recent Literature." *Clergy Review* 49 (November 1964): 687-703.

Sillem briefly reviews modern *Confessions* criticism from its beginnings in 1888 (*see*: **170** and **173**). He suggests that the dust has finally settled on whether Augustine truthfully narrated his conversion scene; most scholars have upheld Augustine's account. Sillem notes the difference between a confession and an autobiography in order to explain Augustine's purpose in writing the *Confessions*. He concludes with a discussion of the Neoplatonist influence question.

078   Solignac, Aimé. "*Introduction aux Confessions*." In *Bibliothèque Augustinienne: Oeuvres de Saint Augustin 13*, 7-226. Paris: Descleé de Brouwer, 1962.

Written in French, this is Solignac's influential review of modern criticism of the *Confessions*. It includes a bibliography of mostly non-English titles.

CULTURAL AND LITERARY ANTECEDENTS

See also: **018, 037, 046, 052, 055, 072, 074-75, 092, 136, 138, 140, 170, 187, 192-93, 223, 237, 243, 251, 254-55, 268, 312, 314, 316, 378, 397, 399, 412, 428, 459**

079   Bennett, Camille. "The Conversion of Vergil: The *Aeneid* in Augustine's *Confessions*." *Revue des Études Augustiniennes* 34 (1988): 47-69.

Bennett argues .hat references to the *Aeneid* in the *Confessions* are part of Augustine's criticism of misguided pagan literature. Relying upon Augustine's earlier analysis of truth and falsehood in literature (*Soliliquies* and *de ordine*), Bennett claims that Augustine determines the truth about the *Aeneid* by reading it spiritually, which amounts to a "conversion" of Virgil.

080 Churchill, Laurie. "*Inopem Me Copia Fecit*: Signs of Narcissus in Augustine's *Confessions*." *Classical and Modern Literature* 10 (Summer 1990): 373-79.

Churchill employs Ovid's version of the Narcissus myth to interpret the *Confessions*. She claims that Augustine's narration of conversion and the story of Narcissus both feature the dynamics of signification in language and the propensity to mistake image for substance.

081 Cochrane, Charles. *Christianity and Classical Culture: A Study of Thought and Action from Augustus to Augustine*. Oxford: Oxford University Press, 1944.

Cochrane claims that Augustinian philosophy (chiefly the invention of personality) fulfills the transition from classical culture to Christianity. He devotes considerable attention to the *Confessions*, its uniqueness as an ancient text, in making the case for the cultural "advancement" that Christians tended to believe they were making.

082 Courcelle, Pierre. *Les Confessions de saint Augustin dans la tradition littéraire: Antécédents et postérité*. Paris: Études Augustiniennes, 1963.

Scholars have disagreed about the uniqueness of the *Confessions*, and its influence in succeeding centuries. A master scholar, Courcelle investigates these two issues. With respect to antecendents, he investigates the *libri Platonicorum* (Platonic books) problem and, once again, Augustine's conversion. With respect to posterity, he only investigates the literary life of Books I-IX over the centuries. That means Courcelle comments only on those texts which quote directly Augustine's text. He is not interested in the history of autobiography, deferring to Misch's work on that issue (**052**).

083 Fichter, Andrew. *Poets Historical: Dynastic Epic in the Renaissance*. New Haven, CT: Yale University Press, 1982.

Fichter reads the *Confessions* as a Christian epic that recapitulates Virgil's *Aeneid*. Rather than found a city, Augustine's Mediteranean travels pertain to personal salvation. Understanding this literary assimilation within the *Confessions* enables one to appreciate the undertakings of epic poets in the Renaissance.

084   Glover, Terrot. *Life and Letters in the Fourth Century.* Cambridge: Cambridge University Press, 1901.

Glover introduces the major literary figures of the fourth century. In a chapter on Augustine, he reviews the *Confessions* up to the time of his conversion (Book VIII).

085   Kuntz, Paul. "Augustine: From *homo erro* to *homo viator.*" *Augustinian Studies* 11 (1980): 79-89.

Kuntz begins by summarizing O'Connell's work (**215**), then argues that Augustine is a Christian Theseus who finds his world a labyrinth. The first nine books of the *Confessions* depict the transition from a life of error to the journey which leads to wisdom (Augustine's Ariadne's thread).

086   O'Meara, John. "Augustine the Artist and the *Aeneid.*" In *John J. O'Meara: Studies in Augustine and Eriugena,* ed. by Thomas Halton, 59-68. Washington: Catholic University of America Press, 1992.

O'Meara claims that Augustine was an "artistic" interpreter and writer, meaning that the writings of others often shines through his own writings (and often in contrary ways). The presence of the *Aeneid* in the *Confessions* demonstrates this aspect of Augustine's authorship.

087   O'Meara, John. "Virgil and Augustine: The *Aeneid* in the *Confessions.*" *Maynooth Review* 13 (1988): 30-43.

O'Meara articulates the sympathy Augustine had for Virgil, then considers several ways in which the *Aeneid* influenced the *Confessions.* Augustine viewed himself as another Aeneas; his youthful preoccupation with love was inspired by the story of Dido; and his conversion followed the pattern of Aeneas's abandonment of Dido. *See also*: **086, 316.**

088   Ottley, Robert. *Studies in the Confessions of St. Augustine.* London: Robert Scott, 1919.

This is a collection of six lectures in which Ottley analyzes major biographical issues raised in the *Confessions* (such as the influence of Manicheism on Augustine). In the last lecture he discusses the place of the *Confessions* in literature and religion.

089   Pucci, Joseph. "The Dilemma of Writing: Augustine, *Confessions*, Book 4.6 and Horace, *Odes*, Book 1.3." *Arethusa* 24 (Fall 1991): 257-81.

The literary element of the *Confessions* has been neglected according to Pucci. Contributing to a remedy, he analyzes an allusion to Horaces *Odes* in

Augustine's recollection of his best friend's death. Pucci concludes that the use of Horace demonstrates Augustine's sensitivity to the moral dilemma entailed in the bold act of writing to God.

090 Ramage, Carol. "The *Confessions* of St. Augustine: The *Aeneid* Revisited." *Pacific Coast Philology* 5 (1970): 54-60.

Augustine never turned his back upon the pagan literature he studied as a child. Instead, he opposed it by transforming it to Christian use. Ramage illustrates this practice by investigating the reappearance of Virgil's *Aeneid* in the *Confessions*.

CULTURAL AND LITERARY INFLUENCE

See also: **001, 004-05, 007, 013-14, 017-18, 020, 036, 043-45, 082-83, 134, 137, 139, 194, 236, 238, 242, 257-58, 260, 306, 309, 316, 320, 338, 340, 344, 358, 421, 428, 436**

091 Abrams, Meyer. *Natural Supernaturalism: Tradition and Revolution in Romantic Literature.* New York: Norton, 1971.

In this classic, Abrams documents the secularization of theological ideas that occurred in the literatures of England and Germany in the decades following the French Revolution. Wordsworth's poetry, particulary his Prospectus for *The Recluse*, serves as Abrams organizing principle. Twice he interprets the *Confessions* of Augustine: first in contrast to Wordsworth's *Prelude*, second in comparing Neoplatonic (and biblical) themes such as the return of the prodigal to romantic ideals.

092 Auerbach, Erich. *Mimesis: The Representation of Reality in Western Literature.* Trans. by Willard Trask. Princeton, NJ: Princeton University Press, 1968.

This is a classic interpretation of European literature from Homer to Proust. Auerbach focuses on a passage from Book VI (about how Augustine's friend Alypius lost the will to resist a gladiatorial show) in his interpretation of the *Confessions*. He demonstrates how rational culture of classical antiquity is swept away in Augustine's more penetrating presentation of the human will.

093 Colish, Marcia. *The Mirror of Language: A Study in the Medieval Theory of Knowledge.* Rev. ed. Lincoln, NE: University of Nebraska Press, 1983.

Colish investigates the common Augustinian conception of words as signs that undergirds medieval thought and informs the differences in medieval epistemologies. She focuses her study on Augustine, Anselm, Aquinas, and Dante. She uses the *Confessions* to organize her discussion of Augustine because it is representative of Augustine's personalistic style of thought. Interpreting the *Confessions* from the point of view of sign theory enables Colish to correlate the autobiographical and theological portions of the text.

094   Disalvo, Angelo. *Reflections of the Theological Tradition of St. Augustine in Cervantes*. Tallahassee, FL: Florida State University, 1981.

Ph.D. dissertation. Disalvo investigates traces of Augustinian theological principles (saving grace, free will, original sin) in Cervantes's writings. He confines his study of Augustine to the *City of God*, *Confessions*, and *On Christian Doctrine*.

095   Fleming, John. "Carthaginian Love: Text and Supertext in the *Roman de la Rose*." In *Assays: Critical Approaches to Medieval and Renaissance Texts*, ed. by Peggy Knapp and Michael Stugrin, 51-72. Pittsburg, PA: University of Pittsburg Press, 1981.

Fleming analyzes a passage from Jean de Meun's poem, *Roman de la Rose*, in which he suggests that love cannot be found in Carthage. Fleming concludes that the passage indicates a "supertextual" presence in the poem, meaning that some other text (in this case, Augustine's *Confessions*) is determining the framework for Jean's poem.

096   Gibson, Joseph. *Babylon Anatomized: Burton's use of Augustine*. Hamilton, ON: McMaster University, 1989.

Ph.D. dissertation. Gibson argues that Burton's *Anatomy of Melancholy* depends upon Augustine's *Confessions* and *City of God*. He claims that Burton's attitude toward the world is a form of Augustinian scepticism.

097   Guitton, Jean. *The Modernity of Saint Augustine*. Trans. by A. V. Littledale. Baltimore: Helicon, 1959.

Interested in demonstating Augustine's relevance for today, Guitton compares Augustine to modern thinkers on the subject of historical existence. In a chapter on the interior life he relies chiefly upon the *Confessions* in making comparisons to Freud, Proust, Gide, and Sartre. He claims that Augustine is a good model for our age which seems to be facing an uncertain future.

098   Haile, H. G. "The Numidian and the German Faustus." *Deutsche Vierteljahrsschrift fur Literaturwissenschaft und Geistesgeschichte* 63 (June 1989): 253-66.

Haile claims that Faust probably entered German literature as a literary symbol rather than as a 16th century historical person. The literary symbolism begins in the *Confessions* with Augustine's mention of the Manichean Faustus of Mileva.

099   Kight, Duane. *From "Secret Cell" to Compostella: Medieval Itineraries of Theosis.* Philadelphia: University of Pennsylvania, 1990.

Ph.D. dissertation. Kight investigates the manner in which medieval writers were able to effect an encounter with God (theosis) by creating an intertextual "secret cell" of biblical authority within their pilgrim writings. He reads the *Confessions* as such an indirect encounter with the divine.

100   Long, Haniel. *A Letter to St. Augustine after Re-reading his Confessions.* New York: Duell, Sloan and Pearce, 1950.

Long comments upon a series of quotations from the *Confessions*, making references to events and literature from all periods of Western civilization. He tries to make Augustine come to life.

101   McGuire, Brian. "Sexual Awareness and Identity in Aelred of Rievaulx (1110-67)." *American Benedictine Review* 45 (June 1994): 184-226.

As response to current claims that Aelred was gay, McGuire investigates his published writings in order to assess Aelred's reasons for entering celibate life. He claims that Aelred did not do so in order to avoid wrestling with his own sexuality. Augustine's *Confessions* is discussed as literary background for *Spiritual Friendship*, *Rule of Life for a Recluse*, and *Mirror of Charity*.

102   Mordell, Albert. *Dante and Other Waning Classics.* Philadelphia: Acropolis Publishing Company, 1915.

Believing that literature should never be a vehicle for theology, Mordell argues that the literary merit of six Christian classics (Dante's *Divine Comedy*, Milton's *Paradise Lost*, Bunyan's *Pilgrim's Progress*, á Kempis's *Imitation of Christ*, Augustine's *Confessions*, and Pascal's *Pensées*) has declined as their theology has become false. He attempts to extract their literary qualities from their obsolete doctrines. Mordell thinks that Augustine's conversion was one of the great calamities of history because Augustine's theology ruined Western civilization.

103   Morrison, Karl. *"I Am You": The Hermeneutics of Empathy in Western Literature, Theology, and Art.* Princeton, NJ: Princeton University Press, 1988.

Morrison defends the tradition of empathic inquiry that modern science scorned and marginalized. The assimilation of self to others, which is the meaning of empathy, is captured by the phrase "I am you." Morrison interprets this phrase as the leitmotif for understanding the enterprise of empathic understanding. He focuses on the *Confessions*, briefly, in order to demonstrate the role of play (or probability) in Western spirituality, and, more broadly, the place of "malevolent sympathy" (or competition) in the game of love.

104   Near, Michael. *The Formal Attire of Being: Self-Consciousness and the Representation of Identity in Augustine's Confessions, the Old English Beowulf, and Chaucer's Troilus.* Berkeley, CA: University of California, 1988.

Ph.D. dissertation. Near claims that medieval self-identity was constituted for specific purposes, which is different than the kind of object-self of today. Augustine's identity, as disclosed in the *Confessions*, is constituted in the power of grace.

105   Paolini, Shirley. "Symbolic-Mythical Space in Dante's *Divina Commedia*, Augustine's *Confessions*, and Eliot's *Waste Land*: The *Regio Dissimilitudinus* Expressed in Desert Spaces, Sea Voyages, and Exodus Figures." In *Proceedings of the XIIth Congress of the International Comparative Literature Association, 2: Space and Boundaries in Literature*, ed. by Roger Bauer and Douwe Fokkema, 565-70. Munich: Iudicium Verlag, 1990.

The lost soul, according to the *Confessions*, falls into a "region of unlikeness" (*regio dissimilitudinus*) that is without illumination. To overcome this darkness, Augustine undertook an arduous spiritual journey that resulted in conversion and self knowledge. Paolini claims that the *Commedia* follows the same pattern, using the same sea voyage metaphor that Augustine borrowed from the Prodigal Son parable. She sees echoes of Augustine's and Dante's region of unlikeness in *The Waste Land*.

106   Shwartz, Susan. "The Founding and Self-Betrayal of Britain: An Augustinian Approach to Geoffrey of Monmouth's *Historia Regum Britanniae*." *Medievalia et Humanistica: Studies in Medieval and Renaissance Culture* 10 (1981): 33-53.

Shwartz argues against those critics who claim that Geoffrey of Monmouth's twelfth century *Historia* was more fable than Christian historiography. She demonstrates that the same historical pattern of betrayal, punishment, exile, and the hope of restoration applies to both the *Confessions* and the *Historia*.

107   Smurthwaite, John. *The Shape of Time: Structure and Conversion in Works of Augustine, Dante, and Petrarch.* Ithaca, NY: Cornell University, 1986.

Ph.D. dissertation. Smurthwaite reads the *Confessions* from the point of view of books X and XI (Augustine's discussions of memory and time), which in his opinion unite the two parts of the text (autobiographical, didactic) and help make sense of conversion experience. Then he interprets Dante and Petrarch as Augustinian thinkers who nevertheless remain committed to their own times.

108   Sutherland, Christine. "Love as Rhetorical Principle: The Relationship Between Content and Style in the Rhetoric of St. Augustine." In *Grace, Politics* *and Desire: Essays on Augustine*, ed. by Hugo Meynell, 139-54. Calgary: University of Calgary, 1990.

Sutherland corrects the mistaken view that Augustine sanctioned the divorce of style from content in rhetoric, thus playing a part in the downfall of that discipline. She demonstrates how *On Christian Doctrine* and the *Confessions* support Augustine's understanding of the place of rhetoric (as means to an end, truth) in the great unity of love.

109   Vander Weele, Michael. *Presence and Judgment in Literary Knowing: A Study of Augustine, Fowles, Fielding and Eliot.* Iowa City, IA: University of Iowa, 1981.

Ph.D. dissertation. Vander Weele develops a theory of relational knowing from his reading of the *Confessions*, then develops it further in readings of other texts.

110   Whelan, Ruth. "The Wage of Sin Is Orthodoxy: The *Confessions* of Saint Augustine in Bayle's *Dictionnaire.*" *Journal of the History of Philosophy* 26 ((April 1988): 195-206.

Bayle was an early champion of anti-religious sentiment in the Enlightenment, or so his 18th century admirers and detractors thought. Whelan reopens the case by attempting to assess more accurately the import of Bayle's biography of Augustine in the *Dictionnaire*. She claims that Bayle both admired and criticised Augustine for good reasons, and that the context of his short biography was quickly overlooked.

111   Wright, Robert. *Art and the Incarnate Word: Medieval Christologies and the Problem of Literary Inexpressibility.* Chapel Hill, NC: Duke University, 1986.

Ph.D. dissertation. Wright demonstrates how Augustine's pessimistic view of the ineffable (expressed in his theory of signs and classically exemplified in the *Confessions*) was overturned in the high Middle Ages.

112   Zacher, Christian. *Curiosity and Pilgrimage: The Literature of Discovery in Fourteenth Century England.* Baltimore: Johns Hopkins University Press, 1976.

Ph.D. dissertation. Zacher examines medieval attitudes surrounding the scriptural antithesis between this world and the next by focusing upon the convergence of two ideas, curiosity and pilgrimage. In the early Middle Ages, curiosity was viewed as temptation and vice, a threat to the Christian practice of travel through the world in order to arrive at sanctified places. By the fourteenth century, however, curiosity dominated pilgrimage, becoming the main motivation for travel. Zacher interprets the *Confessions* briefly as a source for the theological notion that worldly curiosity is evil.

POSTMODERN INTERPRETATION

See also: **038, 269, 280, 305, 388-89, 430, 432, 436**

113 Fendt, Gene. "Confessions Bliss: Postmodern Criticism as a Palimpsest of Augustine's *Confessions*." *Heythrop Journal* 36 (January 1995): 30-45.

According to Roland Barthes, a "text of bliss" is an untenable text that cannot be understood conventionally. Instead, its world of signs and meanings must be rewritten upon, like a palimpsest, which is what Fendt does with the *Confessions* in order to illustrate some of the insights of deconstruction.

114 Ferguson, Margaret. "Saint Augustine's Region of Unlikeness: The Crossing of Exile and Language." *Georgia Review* 29 (1975): 842-64.

Ferguson explores Augustine's Neoplatonic interpretation of fallen existence in the *Confessions*, linking Augustine's pessimistic view of language (human words are essentially "unlike" the divine Word, which makes life an "exile") to Derrida's view that a metaphysical concept of truth as Presence underlies Western thought.

115 Fletcher, Pauline. "Augustine and the Pleasures of the Text." *The CEA Critic* 48 (Winter 1985): 56-61.

Fletcher is intrigued by current interest in the *Confessions*. She claims that the *Confessions* is a book about books, and that Augustine's progress in reading scripture is analogous to the modern literary critic's progress in appreciation for the instability of texts. In both cases, room is made for creative, pleasurable interpretation.

116 Flores, Ralph. "Doubling and the *Speculum aenigmate* in Augustine's *Confessions*." *New Orleans Review* 8 (Fall 1981): 13-22.

By interpreting a series of binary oppositions in the *Confessions*, Flores demonstrates the inability of Augustine to overcome the enigmatic nature of his own conversion.

117 Foster, Dennis. *Confession and Complicity in Narrative*. Cambridge: Cambridge University Press, 1987.

Foster attempts to demonstrate the truthfulness of post-structural theories of writing (texts are determined more by the intertextual world of writing than by authorial intentions) by examining the motives of confessional literature. In his reading of the *Confessions*, he focuses upon Augustine's attempts to control the reader's interpretation. Augustine's narration is actually a deviant solicitation of praise and like-mindedness from others according to Foster.

118 Humphrey, George. *Metamorphoses of Desire: Eden and the Boundaries of Literature*. Boston: Boston University, 1987.

Ph.D. dissertation. Humphrey employs Eden as a complex tropology with which to grasp the nature of literary change. He interprets Augustine's conversion as an Edenic scene, as well as Dante's reunion with Beatrice, Milton's description of Eden, and Derrida's reading of Rousseau's festival.

119 Kiely, Robert. "Angelic Discourse or Unstable Allegory? The Play of the Literal and Figurative in Augustine's *Confessions, The Little Flowers* of St. Francis, and Bunyan's *Pilgrim's Progress.*" *Stanford Literature Review* 5 (Spring-Fall 1988): 105-30.

Kiely disagrees with those who believe that postmodern stories (allegories) are fraught with tensions and ambiguities that premodern religious allegories were spared in their symbolic serenity and naïveté. He focuses upon angelic episodes from three religious classics in order to demonstrate the interpretive uncertainty resident in texts of faith. From the *Confessions*, he employs Augustine's description of Monica's dream of the wooden ruler in Book III. Monica envisioned an angel who assured her that Augustine would eventually come back to the Catholic faith.

120 Kilgour, Maggie. *From Communion to Cannibalism: An Anatomy of Metaphors of Incorporation*. Princeton, NJ: Princeton University Press, 1990.

Structuralist and post-structuralist criticism has focused upon binary oppositions. Kilgour investigates the opposition between inner and outer as a means for understanding oppositional interpretation as such. What is outer or unfamiliar is made part of the inner through various strategies of bodily incorporation. Kilgour's strategy is to analyze the eating metaphors in various texts, including the *Confessions*.

121 Peters, Gerald. *The Mutilating God: Authorship and Authority in the Narrative of Conversion*. Amherst, MA: University of Massachusetts Press, 1993.

Employing Frye's historical stages of writing (hieroglyphic, hieratic, demotic), De Mann's notion that autobiography is a way of reading self-representational texts (including fiction), and Lacan's theory of psychoanalysis, Peters investigates how the idea of conversion has become more internalized as conceptions of self and world have become more differentiated. He argues that the *Confessions* depicts a conversion in language use as Augustine submits himself to the "mutilation" of being written upon by God's text (Genesis).

122   Robbins, Jill. "Prodigal Son and Elder Brother: The Example of Augustine's *Confessions.*" *Genre* 16 (Winter 1983): 317-33.

Robbins interprets Augustine's use of the parable of the prodigal son as an example of the hermeneutical tendency to overlook the negativity of misunderstanding. She claims that Augustine is too quick to assume that the (Jewish) elder brother represents Cain, when he could as easily represent Abraham. Midrashic interpretation, on the other hand, is not so concerned to transcend and purify all the difficulties of a text.

123   Scanlon, Michael. "Augustine and Theology as Rhetoric." *Augustinian Studies* 25 (1994): 37-50.

Scanlon explains how Augustine, often called the first "modern" man, is also relevant to "postmodern" theology. Postmodern fascination with language is still Augustinian in many ways. Scanlon relies upon the *Confessions* and *de doctrina christiana* to make his point. *See also*: **430**.

124   Taylor, Mark. *Erring: A Postmodern A/theology.* Chicago: University of Chicago Press, 1984.

Taylor claims that deconstructive philosophy can help (postmodern) people caught between belief and unbelief to make sense of their religious heritage. He believes that we must come to terms with the death of God and its effects (disappearance of the self, end of history, and closure of the book). His chapter on the disappearance of the self is a deconstructive reading of the *Confessions*.

125   Troup, Calvin. *Temporality, Eternity, and Wisdom: The Rhetoric of Augustine's Confessions.* State College, PA: Pennsylvania State University, 1994.

Ph.D. dissertation. Troup challenges the view that Augustine condemned rhetoric when he embraced philosophy and Christianity. He reads the *Confessions* as a rhetorical document, and finds that Augustine's preoccupation with language parallels the postmodern return of rhetorical interests.

126   Vander Weele, Michael. "Augustine and Interpretation in *On Christian Doctrine* and the *Confessions.*" *The CEA Critic* 47 (Summer 1985): 13-21.

Vander Weele investigates what Augustine might contribute to current rethinking of interpretation theory and, more generally, the relationship between language, reason, and the world. He tries to rehabilitate the notion of presence (relying upon Gadamerian hermeneutics) after first discussing Augustine's theory of signs.

SELECTED BIOGRAPHIES

See also: **110, 161, 310**

127 Battenhouse, Roy. "The Life of St. Augustine." In *A Companion to the Study of St. Augustine*, ed. by Roy Battenhouse, 15-56. New York: Oxford University Press, 1955.

Battenhouse relies upon the *Confessions* as his primary source (until the time of his ordination) in reviewing Augustine's life. First, however, he reflects upon the *Confessions* as a unique biographical text. He takes issue with modern critics who question the authenticity of the *Confessions* in light of apparent discrepancies with the Cassiciacum dialogues.

128 Brown, Peter. *Augustine of Hippo: A Biography*. Berkeley, CA: University of California Press, 1967.

Brown is perhaps the best historical biographer, masterfully placing the reader into Augustine's Mediterranean world. While emphasizing the changes in Augustine's life, he also draws attention to significant cultural influences (such as African legalism) that help explain Augustine's character and personality. In a chapter on the *Confessions*, Brown indicates how important ideal friendship was to Augustine's gifted generation. *See also*: **294**.

129 Chadwick, Henry. *Augustine*. Past Masters. New York: Oxford University Press, 1986.

Chadwick provides a brief, yet learned and lucid introduction to Augustine's intellectual development and theology. In a chapter on the *Confessions*, he illustrates how the last four books repeat on a theological plane the thesis of the first nine: Augustine (like every human) turned from God in pursuit of an illusory happiness, then was recalled to himself by a longing for completeness that was prompted (and satisfied) by God's love.

130 O'Meara, John. *The Young Augustine: The Growth of St. Augustine's Mind up to his Conversion*. New York: Longman's, Green and Company, 1954.

O'Meara relies primarily upon the *Confessions* in this biography of the young Augustine. In an "Introductory Note," he discusses modern criticism of the *Confessions*. He argues that the *Confessions* is a personalized presentation of Augustine's theory of humanity. Helping us to understand that theory (in the context of Augustine's development) is the purpose of *The Young Augustine*.

131   TeSelle, Eugene. *Augustine the Theologian.* New York: Herder and Herder, 1970.

TeSelle analyzes the theology of Augustine by chronologically investigating his major written works. One conclusion he comes to is that Augustine was not a particularly original thinker; another is that he was an occasional thinker (not systematic) who adopted many points of view. In his discussion of the *Confessions*, TeSelle observes that it functions as a kind of first *Retractatio.*

4

Conversion Experience

AMBROSE

See also: **311, 379, 460, 462**

132 Burns, J. "Ambrose Preaching to Augustine: The Shaping of Faith." In *Collectanea Augustiniana: Augustine, Second Founder of the Faith*, ed. by Joseph Schnaubelt and Frederick Van Fleteren, 373-86. New York: Peter Lang, 1990.

Burns investigates the influence of Ambrose on Augustine's conversion to Christianity. Ambrose was a positive influence in that he convinced Augustine of the intelligibility of Christianity, the value of Platonic philosophy, and the significance of scripture. On the other hand, Ambrose's understanding of evil and spiritual reality probably hindered Augustine.

133 Saint-Laurent, George. "Augustine's Hero-Sage-Holy Man: Ambrose of Milan." *Word and Spirit: A Monastic Review* 9 (1987): 22-34.

Saint-Laurent speculates on the relationship between Augustine and Ambrose, particularly the latter's silence about Augustine. On the other hand, Augustine seems to have followed Athanasius's pattern from the *Life of St. Antony* in his depiction of Ambrose in the *Confessions*.

CONTRASTING CONVERSIONS

See also: **087, 105, 118, 157, 282, 373, 391**

134 Chadbourne, Richard. "Two Converts: Augustine and Pascal." In *Grace, Politics and Desire: Essays on Augustine*, ed. by Hugo Meynell, 33-51. Calgary: Calgary University Press, 1990.

Chadbourne articulates the debt Pascal owes Augustine in comparing their conversions, and also Pascal's originality. Pascal shared Augustine's understanding of conversion as response to gratuitous grace. But Pascal was not a philosophical convert like Augustine; he was more Christocentric in outlook, and suffered ill health.

135   Fredriksen, Paula. "Paul and Augustine: Conversion Narratives, Orthodox Traditions and the Retrospective Self." *Journal of Theological Studies* 37 (1986): 3-34.

Why do we construct myriad versions of Paul and Augustine when we try to understand them through their conversions? According to Fredriksen, the problem is traceable to the New Testament's Acts, which convinced us (in part due to Augustine's interpretation and influence) that conversion entails a deliberate turning away from what is old and untrue. She concludes that conversion narratives tend to be apologetic reconstructions, which means that the real historical person can never be found there.

136   Mercedes, Anna. "Two Paths from Plato: Shelley and St. Augustine." *Catholic World* 159 (July 1944): 326-28.

Platonism helped Augustine achieve stability, but it harmed Shelley. Mercedes claims that Shelley saw only dimly what Augustine beheld in unwavering faith. She regrets that Shelley never found faith as Augustine did.

137   Meulman-Young, Sherry. *Coleridge and Conversion: A Reading of The Rime as a Poetic Confession.* Dallas: University of Dallas, 1986.

Ph.D. dissertation. Meulman-Young believes Coleridge's poetry was not so new and modern as is commonly supposed. Instead, she claims that it depended upon classical rhetoric. She reads "The Rime" as poetic confession inspired by Augustine's *Confessions.* In both cases, there is a conversion from forgetfulness to memory.

138   Nock, Arthur. *Conversion: The Old and the New in Religion from Alexander the Great to Augustine of Hippo.* London: Oxford University Press, 1933.

Nock investigates how ancient people were attracted and sometimes converted to religions such as Eastern cults and Christianity. In a final chapter, he contrasts the Christian conversions of Justin, Arnobius and Augustine. Augustine grew up in a world that could take Christianity for granted as a constant background while the other two did not.

139 Wetsel, David. "Augustine's *Confessions*: A Problematic Model for Pascal's Conversion Itinerary in the *Pensées*." *Papers on French Seventeenth Century Literature* 17 (1990): 123-49.

Wetsel argues that the later, more pessimistic Augustine influenced Pascal's reflections upon conversion and apologetics. The *Confessions* (an earlier, optimistic work of Augustine's) do not figure much in Pascal's *Pensées*.

140 Wilson, Anna. "Reason and Revelation in the Conversion Accounts of the Cappadocians and Augustine." In *Collectanea Augustiniana: Mélanges T. J. Van Bavel*, ed. by Bernard Bruning, M. Lamberigts, and J. Van Houtem, 259-78. Leuven: University Press, 1990.

Wilson compares Augustine's conversion account in the Confessions (chiefly) to various writings of Gregory of Nyssa and Gregory of Nazianzen. These men were near contemporaries and shared similar upbringings and educations. Despite their separation as Christians of Western and Eastern persuasions, Wilson remarks upon the similar use of biblical and pagan studies in their thinking. One difference that stands out is the isolation of Augustine compared to the Cappadocians.

CONVERSION ANALYSIS

See also: **030, 116, 121, 187, 200, 289, 293, 364, 422, 441, 451, 464**

141 Brusseau, James. "These Sober Pages." *Literature and Theology* 5 (June 1991): 151-61.

Brusseau offers a meditation on sober themes (evil, nothing, finitude, fallenness, parody) in order to demonstrate the radical nature of Augustine's transformation in the *Confessions*. He becomes something completely new and different, which is hard to portray in writing.

142 Coward, Harold. "Memory and Scripture in the Conversion of Augustine." In *Grace, Politics and Desire: Essays on Augustine*, ed. by Hugo Meynell, 19-30. Calgary: University of Calgary Press, 1990.

Coward claims that Augustine's conversion is best understood in terms of the dynamics of memory and scripture. Coward's psychological analysis is based upon readings of the *Confessions* and *de trinitate*. By memorizing scriptural passages, Augustine internalized the voice of God which later enabled him to remember and return to God.

143 Desmond, William. "Augustine's *Confessions*: On Desire, Conversion and Reflection." *Irish Theological Quarterly* 47 (1980): 24-33.

Desmond is struck by the coincidence of reflection and experience in the *Confessions*. He contrasts Augustine's style of thought (seeking satisfaction of desire through conversion) to Aquinas's (seeking clarification of faith already attained).

144 Guardini, Romano. *The Conversion of Augustine*. Trans. by E. Briefs. Westminster, MD: Newman Press, 1960.

Guardini clarifies how best to interpret the *Confessions*, presenting Augustine's personality and thought as a real possibility of Christian existence. He criticises interpreters who focus only upon moral, psychological, or historical issues, which ignore the coherence and logic of the life of faith Augustine wrote about.

145 Martin, Thomas. "The Conversion of St. Augustine: 1600 Years in Retrospect." *Review for Religious* 45 (September-October 1986): 701-08.

Martin articulates the direction (and challenge) that Augustine's conversion can provide contemporary Christians. Like Augustine, we are called to an inward journey that leads to the Other and others.

146 Matter, E. "Conversion(s) in the *Confessiones*." In *Collectanea Augustiniana: Augustine, Second Founder of the Faith*, ed. by Joseph Schnaubelt and Frederick Van Fleteren, 21-28. New York: Peter Lang, 1990.

Matter analyzes Augustine's use of conversion narrative in light of modern scholarship on the nature of religious conversion. She claims that we must attend to the *Confessions* themselves in order to understand what Augustine meant by conversion.

147 O'Brien, William. "The Liturgical Form of Augustine's Conversion Narrative and its Theological Significance." *Augustinian Studies* 9 (1978): 45-58.

Enframing the conversion narrative in Book VIII of the *Confessions* is a gospel passage (Matthew 11:25-29) and a psalm passage (115:7). O'Brien finds similar scriptural references in one of Augustine's sermons, which leads him to speculate about what Augustine was attempting to show the reader in telling his story in such an artful fashion.

148 Somerville, James. "The Preludes to Conversion in the Philosophy of St. Augustine." *The Modern Schoolman* 21 (May 1944): 191-203.

The proper balance of reason and faith is the philosophical issue in religious conversion according to Somerville. He demonstrates how this is true for Augustine, whose experiential philosophy was rooted in his faith.

149   Stark, Judith. "The Dynamics of the Will in Augustine's Conversion." In *Collectanea Augustiniana: Augustine: Second Founder of the Faith*, ed. by Joseph Schnaubelt and Frederick Van Fleteren. New York: Peter Lang, 1990.

Stark closely analyzes the stages through which Augustine's understanding of the will moves, from an initial recognition of how difficult habits are to break to the point where his old loves have been transformed into new ones with God's help.

150   Underwood, Alfred. *Conversion, Christian and Non-Christian: A Comparative and Psychological Study*. London: Allen and Unwin, 1925.

Underwood presents a study of conversion from two standpoints: history of religions and psychology. His most extensive interpretation of the *Confessions* pertains to the psychological mechanism of conversion. Augustine represents the type of conversion in which a personal crisis is resolved by choosing one line of conduct as opposed to another.

151   Van Fleteren, Frederick. "St. Augustine's Theory of Conversion." In *Collectanea Augustiniana: Augustine, Second Founder of the Faith*, ed. by Joseph Schnaubelt and Frederick Van Fleteren, 65-80. New York: Peter Lang, 1990.

Following the standards of form criticism, Van Fleteren describes fifteen elements that typically appear in the dozen different conversion stories found in the *Confessions*.

FICTION THESIS

See also: **028, 033, 042, 064, 077, 082, 147, 166-67, 169-71, 175-76**

152   Archambault, Paul. "Shifts of Narrative Level in Saint Augustine's *Confessions*." *Augustinian Studies* 17 (1986): 109-17.

Archambault studes two subnarratives that depict other points of view than Augustine's in books VII and VIII of the *Confessions*. The subnarratives prefigure the garden scene in which Augustine describes his conversion. Archambault concludes that such stylized narrative construction lends support to Courcelle's fictional thesis (**153**).

153   Courcelle, Pierre. *Recherches sur les Confessions de saint Augustin*. Paris: E. de Boccard, 1950.

Perhaps the greatest Augustine scholar of the century, Courcelle thinks that much of the controversy over Augustine's conversion (whether the *Confessions* provides a fictional account, whether Augustine was a Neoplatonist or Christian) is the result of theological bias on the part of modern critics. He interprets the *Confessions* from a philological or literary-historical perspective instead, and concludes that the garden scene is largely fictional. Includes an extensive bibliography of mostly non-English titles.

154 Ferrari, Leo. "An Analysis of Augustine's Conversional Reading." *Augustinian Studies* 18 (1987): 30-51.

Ferrari employs his biblical citation method to support the thesis that the conversion scene in Book VIII is largely fictional. He finds no evidence for Augustine's awareness of the passage in Romans that he claims to have read in the garden at Milan. *See also*: **155-58**.

155 Ferrari, Leo. "Beyond Augustine's Conversion Scene." In *Augustine: From Rhetor to Theologian*, ed. by Joanne McWilliam, 97-107. Waterloo, ON: Wilfrid Laurier University Press, 1992.

First, Ferrari reviews his conclusion (based on previous analysis of Augustine's biblical citations) that the conversion scene is fictional (**156-57**). Then he investigates two related problems: how Augustine's honesty can be defended even though he fictionalized his conversion; and what the real conversion behind the fictional account must have been like.

156 Ferrari, Leo. "Paul at the Conversion of Augustine." *Augustinian Studies* 11 (1980): 5-20.

Ferrari reviews the debate between historicists and fictionalists concerning the conversion scene in Book VIII of the *Confessions*. Then he looks more carefully at Augustine's discovery of St. Paul's letters, comparing the *Confessions* account to other written accounts. He concludes that the *tolle lege* scene is a fictional composite based in part upon an earlier experience of Pauline discovery. *See also*: **154-55, 157-58**.

157 Ferrari, Leo. "Saint Augustine on the Road to Damascus." *Augustinian Studies* 13 (1982): 151-70.

Ferrari argues that Augustine's conversion scene in Book VIII of the *Confessions* is dependent upon St. Paul's conversion on the road to Damascus as told in *Acts*. His investigation of the similarities between the two conversions provides further evidence for his fictional thesis regarding Augustine's conversion. *See also*: **154-56, 158**.

158 Ferrari, Leo. "Saint Augustine's Conversion Scene: The End of a Modern Debate?" In *Studia Patristica* 22, ed. by Elizabeth Livingstone, 235-50. Leuven: Peeters Press, 1989.

Ferrari reviews the modern debate over the historicity of Augustine's conversion, begun in 1888 by Harnack (170) and Boissier (167). Then he defends his own fictional interpretation of the conversion scene as first presented in other articles (156, 157). He is convinced that the modern debate arose from misunderstanding the dramatic nature of the *Confessions*.

159   Ferrari, Leo. "Truth and Augustine's Conversion Scene." In *Collectanea Augustiniana: Augustine: Second Founder of the Faith*, ed. by Joseph Schnaubelt and Frederick Van Fleteren, 9-19. New York: Peter Lang, 1990.

How can Augustine's regard for the truth be reconciled with the fictional account of his own conversion? The answer, according to Ferrari, is Augustine's high regard for figurative language.

160   Mohrmann, Christine. "The *Confessions* as a Literary Work of Art." *Études sur le latin des chrétiens* 1 (1958): 378-81.

Mohrmann responds to Courcelle's claim that the conversion narrative in Book VIII of the *Confessions* is probably a literary construction rather than an historical account of events (153). Relying upon an analysis of Augustine's narrative-meditative style, she argues that the conversion scene is meant to be factually correct.

161   Montgomery, W. *St. Augustine: Aspects of His Life and Thought.* New York: Hodder and Stoughton, 1914.

In one of the lenten lectures comprising this book, Montgomery reviews the modern controversy concerning Augustine's conversion (whether his *Confessions* account is accurate), and finds it to be a minor distraction of little merit.

162   O'Meara, John. "'*Arripui, aperui, et legi*' (*Confessions* VIII, 12, 29)." In *Augustinus Magister I: Congrès International Augustinien, 1954*, ed. by Fulbert Cayré, 59-65. Paris: Études Augustiniennes, 1954.

O'Meara challenges Courcelle's argument that the conversion scene described in Book VIII of the *Confessions* never happened (153). He shows how Augustine recalls the scene in other writings, which indicates the likelihood that it was real rather than fictional.

163   O'Meara, John. "Augustine's *Confessions*: Elements of Fiction." In *Augustine: From Rhetor to Theologian*, ed. by Joanne McWilliam, 77-95. Waterloo, ON: Wilfrid Laurier University Press, 1992.

Leaving aside the question of the historicity of the *Confessions*, O'Meara investigates the many fictional techniques that Augustine uses in telling his moral tale.

MULTIPLE CONVERSIONS

See also: 079, 151, 155, 176, 179, 213, 222, 338, 396

164   Ferrari, Leo. *The Conversions of Saint Augustine*. The Saint Augustine Lecture, 1982. Villanova, PA: Villanova University Press, 1984.

Ferrari discusses three conversions (or transformations) reported in the *Confessions*: Augustine's conversions to Neoplatonic philosophy, Manicheism, and Catholicism. The conversion to Catholicism is further broken into two stages: the *tolle, lege* scene which leads to Augustine's baptism, and the maturation of his thought following that.

165   Markus, Robert. *Conversion and Disenchantment in Augustine's Spiritual Career*. The Saint Augustine Lecture, 1987. Villanova, PA: Villanova University Press, 1989.

Markus evaluates four upheavals or "conversions" in Augustine's life, three of which involve disenchantment with a previous perspective. He emphasizes the continuity in Augustine's spiritual career, bemoaning the too numerous studies that focus only upon textual discrepancies in the *Confessions* concerning his "conversion" to Christianity from Neoplatonism.

TWO AUGUSTINE'S THEORY

See also: 003, 127, 153, 158, 161-62, 164-65

166   Alfaric, Prosper. *L'Evolution intellectuelle de saint Augustin: Du Manichéisme au Néoplatonisme*. Paris: E. Nourry, 1918.

In this influential work, Alfaric pushes modern criticism of the *Confessions* to an extreme by arguing that Augustine was converted to Neoplatonism, not Christianity, in 386 AD.

167   Boissier, Gaston. "La conversion de saint Augustin." *Revue des deux mondes* 85 (1888): 43-69.

Boissier was the first to propose a "two Augustine's" theory, which inaugurated modern *Confessions* criticism (*see also*: 170). Comparing Augustine's conversion account in the *Confessions* (written ten or more years afterwards) with the Cassiciacum dialogues (written at the time of conversion) reveals discrepancies that call into question Augustine's accuracy in the *Confessions*.

168 Crouse, Robert. *"In Aenigmate Trinitas* (*Confessions*, 13.5.6): The Conversion of Philosophy in St. Augustine's *Confessions.*" *Dionysius* 11 (December 1987): 53-62.

According to Crouse, it is not possible to separate Augustine's Platonism from his Christianity. After his Christian conversion, he did not drop Platonic philosophy; instead, he converted it along with the rest of his life.

169 Garvey, Mary. *Saint Augustine: Christian or Neo-Platonist? From His Retreat at Cassiciacum until His Ordination at Hippo.* Milwaukee: Marquette University Press, 1939.

Ph.D. dissertation. Earlier writings by Augustine suggest that he was converted to Neoplatonism rather than Christianity in 386 AD, which seems to contradict the conversion narrative of the *Confessions.* Garvey reviews the literature pertaining to this problem of modern criticism, then proposes a solution that is based upon a more careful understanding of what differentiates Christianity from Neoplatonism. While Augustine tended to speak in Neoplatonic terms, he was essentially a Christian thinker according to Garvey.

170 Harnack, Adolf von. *Monasticism and The Confessions of Saint Augustine.* Trans. by E. E. Kellett and F. H. Marseille. New York: G. Putnam's Sons, 1910.

Harnack's lecture on the *Confessions,* delivered in 1888, helped to inaugurate modern *Confessions* criticism (*see also*: **167**). He discusses the unique form and style of Augustine's text in ancient literature before turning to issues of content. He compares the *Confessions* to Goethe's *Faust* (*see also*: **098**). In retelling the tale of Augustine's conversion, he "corrects" the *Confessions* narrative with reference to the Cassiciacum dialogues.

171 Henry, Paul. "Augustine and Plotinus." *The Journal of Theological Studies* 38 (1937): 1-23.

Henry documents Augustine's lifelong respectful attitude toward Plotinus: at the time of his conversion (Cassiciacum dialogues), early in his career as bishop (*Confessions*), and later in life (*City of God*). He discounts the trend in modern criticism to dispute the historicity of the *Confessions* (was Augustine really converted to Christianity, or Neoplatonism?) by comparison to the Cassiciacum dialogues. He argues that Plotinus's *Enneads* are the "Platonic books" referred to in Book VII of the *Confessions.*

172 Kevane, Eugene. "Christian Philosophy: The Intellectual Side of Augustine's Conversion." *Augustinian Studies* 17 (1986): 47-83.

Kevane views Augustine's conversion as the beginning point of a uniquely Christian philosophy that brought Greek and Roman humanism into the educational program of medieval culture. He briefly reviews the modern controversy concerning Augustine's conversion, and claims that it resulted from an inability to recognize the uniqueness of Augustine's Christian philosophy.

173   Kevane, Eugene. "Philosophy, Education, and the Controversy on St. Augustine's Conversion." *Studies in Philosophy and History of Philosophy* 2 (1963): 61-103.

Kevane argues that the modern controversy about Augustine's conversion (was he converted to Christianity or Neoplatonism?) is based upon a misunderstanding of his purpose at Cassiciacum, which was to develop a Christian philosophy of education. He believes that his explanation of Augustine's pedagogical purpose will resolve the controversy in favor of the historicity of the *Confessions* narrative. Kevane's article includes an extensive review of modern *Confessions* criticism on this issue.

174   Mallard, William. "The Incarnation in Augustine's Conversion." *Recherches Augustiniennes* 15 (1980): 80-98.

Mallard determines the role that Neoplatonism played in Augustine's conversion by investigating his understanding of the Christian doctrine of Incarnation. He claims two things: first, that Augustine's affirmation of the Incarnation repudiates prior Neoplatonists and, second, that Augustine's understanding of the eternal mercy disclosed by the word-made-flesh is itself a new version of Platonizing thought.

175   McGuckin, John. "The Enigma of Augustine's Conversion: September 386 AD." *Clergy Review* 71 (September 1986): 315-25.

McGuckin reviews Augustine's development up to the point of his conversion, then he discusses the controversy surrounding Augustine's account of the conversion in the *Confessions*. He explains how Augustine may have reconstructed events for pedagogical purposes. McGuckin concludes his essay with a brief look at Augustine's baptism, which was also emotionally significant.

176   O'Connell, Robert. "On Augustine's 'First Conversion': *Factus Erectior* (*de beata vita* 4)." *Augustinian Studies* 17 (1986): 15-29.

O'Connell investigates Augustine's first conversion to philosophy described in books III and VIII of the *Confessions*. He compares that account to one given in the prologue to the Cassiciacum dialogue, *de beata vita*. Against Courcelle (**170**), O'Connell argues that Augustine did not stay with the philosophical path because he was raised up (*factus erectior*) to something more noble.

177 O'Connell, Robert. "The Visage of Philosophy at Cassiciacum."
Augustinian Studies 25 (1994): 86-104.

O'Connell takes a new look at the "two Augustine's" controversy by comparing
once again the *Confessions* and the Cassiciacum dialogues. He concludes that
the parallels between the *Confessions* and dialogues outweigh the discrepancies:
If there are two Augustine's, he says, they are twins. *See also*: **167**.

178 O'Meara, John. "Neoplatonism in the Conversion of Saint Augustine."
Dominican Studies 3 (1950): 331-43.

O'Meara compares the *Confessions* to the *Contra Academicos* (one of the
Cassiciacum dialogues) in order to refute the modern critical claim that
Augustine was converted to Neoplatonism in 386 AD, not to Christianity as he
reports in the *Confessions*.

179 Pegis, Anton. "The Second Conversion of St. Augustine." In *Gesellschaft,
Kultur, Literatur: Rezeption und Originalität im Wachsen einer Europäischen
Literatur und Geistigkeit*, ed. by Karl Bosl, 79-93. Stuttgart: Anton Hiersemann,
1975.

Focusing upon Book X, which depicts Augustine's state of mind when he was
writing the *Confessions*, Pegis reflects upon the growth Augustine had realized
since his initial conversion a dozen years earlier. This growth constitutes the
"second conversion" of Augustine, which enabled him to transform the synthesis
of Neoplatonist philosophy and biblical faith into a permanent doctrine of the
church.

180 Russell, Robert. "Cicero's *Hortensius* and the Problem of Riches in Saint
Augustine." *Augustinian Studies* 7 (1976): 59-68.

Russell investigates the influence of Cicero upon Augustine's conversion to
philosophy, particularly the renunciation of his desire for riches. He compares a
statement from the *Soliloquies*, which indicates that Cicero's *Hortensius*
persuaded him to give up the desire for wealth, with later statements from the
Confessions and *de utulitate credendi*, which indicate that he did not give up the
desire for wealth at the time he read *Hortensius*.

181 Simpson, W. *St. Augustine's Conversion: An Outline of his Development
to the Time of his Ordination*. New York: The Macmillan Company, 1930.

This is one of the early critical assessments of Augustine's intellectual
development, taking into account the modern practice of assessing the
autobiographical record of the *Confessions* against other writings. Simpson
sides with those who affirm the Christian nature of Augustine's conversion. Yet

he argues that a gradual process of intellectual development was required as well.

182   Sweeney, Leo. "'Was St. Augustine a Neoplatonist or a Christian?': Old Question, New Approach." In *Collectanea Augustiniana: Augustine: Second Founder of the Faith*, ed. by Joseph Schnaubelt and Frederick Van Fleteren, 403-20. New York: Peter Lang, 1990.

The old question is whether Augustine was converted to Christianity as suddenly as indicated in the *tolle, lege* scene of the *Confessions*. Instead of comparing texts written by Augustine at different times (the old solution to the old question), Sweeney tries to articulate the essence of Christianity and then judge whether Augustine's *Confessions* fits.

183   Warfield, Benjamin. "Augustine and His *Confessions*." *The Princeton Theological Review* 3 (1905): 81-126.

Warfield provides an early English-language response to modern criticism of the *Confessions*. He admits that Augustine may have exaggerated his past misdeeds, but thinks that the real problem stems from misreading the *Confessions* as a strict autobiographical text, which it is not. He takes up the problem of Augustine's conversion, and responds similarly (pointing out misinterpretations resident in modern criticism).

5

Time and Other Philosophical Issues

AESTHETICS

See also: **039, 086, 103, 111, 115, 320**

184 O'Connell, Robert. *Art and the Christian Intelligence in St. Augustine.* Cambridge, MA: Harvard University Press, 1978.

O'Connell demonstrates the strategic role that art, beauty, and aesthetics played at the inception of Augustine's thought, and in its gradual development. He claims that the *Confessions* substantially confirms the theory of art proposed in the earlier *de musica*. Later, O'Connell investigates the artistry of the *Confessions*, which leads to questions about Augustine's theory of art, and its suitability today.

ETHICS

See also: **010, 056-57, 089, 155, 159, 163, 223-24, 244, 247, 308, 348, 372, 383, 433, 448-50**

185 Kuntz, Paul. "The I-Thou Relation and Aretaic Divine Command Ethics: Augustine's Study of Virtues and Vices in the *Confessions*." *Augustinian Studies* 16 (1984): 107-27.

Kuntz reviews Augustine's presentation of virtues and vices in the *Confessions*, characterizing his point of view as "aretaic [i.e., concerned with *arete* or excellence] divine command ethics." His purpose is to reflect upon the intimate, necessary connection between religion and morality for Augustine. Referring to James's distinction between once and twice born believers (**303**), Kuntz thinks that people like Augustine (twice born) cannot live moral lives without theological warrant, while people like Aquinas (once born) can.

186   Quinn, John. "Anti-Manichean and Other Moral Precisions in *Confessions* 3.7.12-9.17." *Augustinian Studies* 19 (1988): 165-94.

Quinn evaluates Augustine's mini-treatise on the essentials of morality in Book III. The context is Augustine's defense of Old Testament patriarchal behaviors against the Manichean charge of moral relativism. Quinn finds the mini-treatise overly brief in comparison to the later mini-treatise on the nature of time for example (Book XI).

187   Simpson, Dean. "Epicureanism in the *Confessions* of St. Augustine." *Augustinian Studies* 16 (1984): 39-48.

Simpson explores the legacy of Epicurus that, surprisingly, appears in Book VI of the *Confessions*. Most Church Fathers felt only contempt for Epicureanism. Augustine's desire to convert all of pagan culture led him to incorporate all of intellectual history into his writings according to Simpson.

188   Thompson, Christopher. *Augustine and Narrative Ethics*. Marquette, WI: Marquette University, 1994.

Ph.D. dissertation. Why do so many contemporary narrative ethicists appeal to Augustine's *Confessions*? Thompson investigates that question, arguing that a useful theology of creation is implied in Augustine's text.

189   Werpehowski, William. "Weeping at the Death of Dido: Sorrow, Virtue, and Augustine's *Confessions*." *Journal of Religious Ethics* 19 (Spring 1991): 175-91.

Werpehowski reflects ethically and theologically upon the nature of sorrow over the loss of a loved one. His insights are illustrated by reference to literary patterns in the *Confessions*, chiefly Augustine's identification with Aeneas (and, likewise, Monica's with Dido). He thinks Monica's sorrow when Augustine/Aeneas leaves Carthage represents an alternative subtext to the dominant sorrow pattern of detachment illustrated by Augustine's weeping at Monica's (Dido's) death.

190   Williams, Rowan. "'Good for Nothing'?: Augustine on Creation." *Augustinian Studies* 25 (1994): 9-24.

Relying chiefly upon the *Confessions*, Williams responds to the new environmental theology that has lost patience with an Augustinian model of creation. He claims that Augustine's teaching is still relevant because it implies a noninstrumental capacity to love what is other. For Augustine, creation is "good for nothing" only in the sense of being noninstrumental in God's life.

MEMORY

See also: **006, 008, 012, 024, 047, 107, 137, 142, 256, 261, 399, 415, 456**

191 Bourke, Vernon. *Augustine's Love of Wisdom: An Introspective Philosophy.* West Lafayette, IN: Purdue University Press, 1992.

Bourke introduces the philosophy of Augustine by carefully analyzing the first thirty chapters from Book X of the *Confessions.* He believes that these chapters on the nature of memory summarize the main features of Augustine's thought, chiefly the satisfaction of desire (for wisdom, happiness, love, truth, immortality) through the discovery of God within the mind and its mysterious recesses (memory).

192 Breyfogle, Todd. "Memory and Imagination in Augustine's *Confessions.*" *New Blackfriars* 75 (April 1994): 210-23.

Reflecting upon the discussion of memory in Book X, Breyfogle makes the point that Augustine stands within Platonic tradition because he believes that God and truth are resident within memory. Breyfogle also analyzes the shift in Augustine's understanding of imagination between the time when he wrote the *Confessions* and *de vera religione.*

193 Bubacz, Bruce. "Augustine's Account of Factual Memory." *Augustinian Studies* 6 (1975): 181-92.

Relying primarily upon the *Confessions* and *de trinitate,* Bubacz demonstrates the plausibility of Augustine's analysis of memory. He defends Augustine against classical scepticism, and also against those who argue that Augustine's memory reports are never about their ostensible objects.

194 Crouse, Robert. *"In Multa Defluximus: Confessions* X, 29-43, and St. Augustine's Theory of Personality." In *NeoPlatonism and Early Christian Thought: Essays in Honour of A. H. Armstrong,* ed. by H. Blumenthal and Robert Markus, 180-85. London: Variorum Publications, 1981.

Crouse investigates Augustine's doctrine of human personality conceived in trinitarian terms (memory, intellect, will). He claims that Augustine is not the first to conceive the human self in personal terms, though his tri-personal conception has exercised strong influence on Western culture.

195 Mourant, John. *Saint Augustine on Memory.* The Saint Augustine Lecture, 1979. Villanova, PA: Villanova University, 1980.

Mourant provides detailed discussion of Augustine's conception of memory in the *Confessions* and *de trinitate*. He makes distinctions between sensible memory and intellectual memory, as well as memory of self and memory of God. This monograph includes appendices on Augustinian psychology and the unity of the *Confessions*.

196   Prufer, Thomas. "Notes for a Reading of Augustine, *Confessions*, Book X." *Interpretation: A Journal of Political Philosophy* 10 (May-September 1982): 197-200.

Prufer contrasts Aristotle and Augustine on philosophical and theological forms of mind. For Augustine, mindfulness and its choices are manifest out of a prior silent unity with God.

NATURE OF PHILOSOPHY

See also: **020, 081, 126, 148, 172-73, 196, 240, 273, 374, 437, 442**

197   DiLorenzo, Raymond. "Ciceronianism and Augustine's Conception of Philosophy." *Augustinian Studies* 13 (1982): 171-76.

How could Augustine look to authority as the basis of his faith rather than to reason (as Greek philosophy would require)? DiLorenzo argues that Cicero's less exalted understanding of reason, particularly its responsiveness to persuasion and authority, enabled Augustine to overcome the influence of Neoplatonic philosophy in his turn to the authority of scripture and church.

198   Flood, Emmet. *Philosophy and Narrative Form.* Austin, TX: University of Texas, 1986.

Ph.D. dissertation. Flood reads Augustine's *Confessions* and Descartes's *Meditations* in order to demonstrate his claim that philosophy impoverished itself by avoiding non-temporal modes of discourse which reflect the exigencies of life.

199   Hartle, Ann. *Death and the Disinterested Spectator: An Inquiry into the Nature of Philosophy.* Albany, NY: State University of New York Press, 1986.

Hartle offers interpretations of Plato's *Phaedo*, Augustine's *Confessions*, and Descartes's *Discourse on Method* as she questions philosophy's claim to console in the face of death. She concludes that consolation, or preparation for death, is philosophy's only contribution. In reading the *Confessions*, Hartle places Augustine between two kinds of certainty: Socrates' certainty about the immortality of his soul, and Descartes's certainty about his existence.

200   Keiser, R. "Inaugurating Postcritical Philosophy: A Polanyian Meditation on Creation and Conversion in Augustine's *Confessions.*" *Zygon* 22 (Spring 1987): 317-37.

Polanyi tried to forge a new understanding of scientific knowing in *Personal Knowledge* (Routledge, 1958). Keiser attempts to draw out the theological implications of Polanyi's philosophy by investigating Augustine's reflections on creation in the *Confessions*. He also attempts to clarify the relation between conversion and creation, thus answering the question about why Augustine ends his autobiography with a meditation on Genesis.

201   Kuntz, Paul. "St. Augustine's Quest for Truth: The Adequacy of a Christian Philosophy." *Augustinian Studies* 13 (1982): 1-22.

Kuntz describes eight different stages of Augustine's quest for truth as told in the Confessions. He thinks that Augustine's quest is more adequate than modern attempts to define truth empirically or rationally. All the methods of philosophy (existentialism, pragmatism, historicism, etc.) are represented in Augustine's arduous quest.

202   Mourant, John. "Saint Augustine's Quest for Truth." *The New Scholasticism* 5 (July 1931): 206-18.

Mourant contrasts the philosophical or intellectual pursuit of truth, which inevitably leads to scepticism, and the religious pursuit of truth. Only the latter, he claims, can achieve the certainty which is lacking in modern philosophical circles. He uses Augustine's writings (the *Confessions* and other texts) to demonstrate both avenues to truth.

NEOPLATONIST INFLUENCE

See also: 077, 082, 114, 132, 168, 171, 174, 176, 179, 192, 197, 246, 258, 264, 266, 359, 417, 425, 429, 465, 467

203   Armstrong, Hilary. "Spiritual or Intelligible Matter in Plotinus and St. Augustine." In *Augustinus Magister I: Congrès International Augustinien, 1954*, ed. by Fulbert Cayré, 277-83. Paris: Études Augustiniennes, 1954.

Armstrong explains how Augustine appropriated Plotinus's doctrine of intelligible matter in his explication of creation (*Confessions* Book XII, *de genesi ad litteram* Book I). For Plotinus, intelligible matter was thought to be good, not evil, as with sensible matter. Armstrong claims that the gap between Augustine and Plotinus was not great.

204   Armstrong, Hilary. *St. Augustine and Christian Platonism.* The Saint Augustine Lecture, 1966. Villanova, PA: Villanova University Press, 1967.

What kind of Christian Platonist was Augustine? Armstrong compares pagan Platonism, Christian Platonism, and Augustine on three topics (divinity of the soul, goodness of the body, and God's will to save humanity) in order to answer this question. He thinks that the third topic in particular distinguishes Augustine from the Platonists. *See also*: **210**.

205   Barkovich, Greg. "A Reflection on Saint Augustine's *Confessions*." *Gnosis* 3 (December 1990): 111-16.

Barkovich reflects upon Augustine's depiction of his spiritual pilgrimage in the first seven books of the *Confessions*, where the Plotinian themes of return and ascent are prominent.

206   Callahan, John. *Augustine and the Greek Philosophers*. The Saint Augustine Lecture, 1964. Villanova, PA: Villanova University Press, 1967.

Callahan's lecture has three parts: first, he discusses the ontological argument in Greek philosophy, Augustine, and Anselm; second, he discusses the flight of the soul in Greek philosophy and Augustine; third, he discusses time in Greek philosophy and Augustine. In all three parts, particularly the third, the *Confessions* is an important primary source. *See also*: **210**.

207   Gilson, Etienne. *The Christian Philosophy of Saint Augustine*. Trans. by L. E. Lynch. New York: Random House, 1960.

Gilson does not offer sustained interpretation of the *Confessions* in this important systematic work. He does claim, however, that Augustine could not accept a fallen soul doctrine (Origenist or Plotinian) and remain consistent in his biblical conviction about the goodness of life. Gilson's argument has influenced *Confessions* scholarship; *see also*: **214**.

208   Holte, Ragnar. "Faith and Interiority in S. Augustine's *Confessions*." In *Interiorità e Intenzionalità in S. Agostino*, ed. by Antonio Pieretti, 71-83. Rome: Institutum Patristicum Augustinianum, 1990.

Holte discusses the influence of Neoplatonism on Augustine's inward turn of faith. He explains how the theory of time in the *Confessions* supports faith's objective to achieve eternal peace.

209   Matthews, Alfred. *The Development of St. Augustine from Neo-Platonism to Christianity, 386-391 A.D.* Washington: University Press of America, 1980.

In 386 Augustine was converted to Christianity, and in 391 he was ordained to the priesthood. Matthews investigates Augustine's spiritual development during this period by studying the *Confessions* and other early writings. He is interested in Augustine's use of philosophy, though he does not focus upon the question of whether he was Neoplatonist or Christian. Matthews views Augustine as a kind of existentialist.

210 O'Brien, Denis. "Two Readings of St. Augustine." *New Blackfriars* 50 (September 1969): 642-48.

O'Brien criticises two Villanova University lectures that concern Augustine's conversion to Neoplatonism as discussed in Book VII of the *Confessions*. He disputes Callahan's conclusions (**206**) and thinks Armstrong's lecture lacks rigor (**204**).

211 O'Connell, Robert. "Augustine's Rejection of the Fall of the Soul." *Augustinian Studies* 4 (1973): 1-32.

O'Connell responds to criticisms of his thesis that the early Augustine viewed the human as a "fallen soul," and that this view is implicit in the *Confessions*.

212 O'Connell, Robert. "Faith, Reason, and Ascent to Vision in St. Augustine." *Augustinian Studies* 21 (1990): 83-126.

This is O'Connell's belated response to Van Fleteren's publications concerning Augustine's philosophical development (**225, 440**). With respect to the *Confessions*, their dispute concerns Augustine's initial conversion to Neoplatonism as discussed in Book VII. Which Neoplatonists influenced Augustine? According to O'Connell, it was Plotinus; according to Van Fleteren, Plotinus and Porphyry. O'Connell defends his prior published position (**214-15**).

213 O'Connell, Robert. "Isaiah Mothering God in Augustine's *Confessions*." *Thought: A Review of Culture and Idea* 58 (1983): 91-110.

In Book VII of the *Confessions*, Augustine recounts his intellectual conversion that was instigated by reading Platonist books. At a critical point, Augustine confesses to God, *fovisti caput nescientis*. O'Connell argues that the verb *fovere* (to caress or mother) refers to mother images in the Bible, particularly Isaiah. He concludes that Augustine's view of the fallen soul is consistent with his earlier writings, and that the conversion in Book VII is not merely intellectual.

214 O'Connell, Robert. "The Plotinian Fall of the Soul in St. Augustine." *Traditio: Studies in Ancient and Medieval History, Thought and Religion* 19 (1963): 1-35.

O'Connell makes the case that Augustine accepted Plotinus's fallen soul doctrine in his early works, including the *Confessions*. He begins by rebutting Gilson's claim (**207**) that Augustine rejected Origen's portrayal of the universe as a place of punishment, which implies that Augustine could not then uphold Plotinus's fallen soul without inconsistency. O'Connell argues that Augustine and Plotinus view the soul as a mixture of fault and goodness.

215 O'Connell, Robert. *St. Augustine's Confessions: The Odyssey of Soul* 2nd ed. New York: Fordham University Press, 1989.

This is a sequel to *St. Augustine's Early Theory of Man, A.D. 386-391*, confirming the hypothesis that Augustine's early anthropology is essentially Plotinian. The introduction includes a good survey of modern *Confessions* criticism (*see also*: **417**).

216 O'Connell, Robert. "Where the Difference Still Lies." *Augustinian Studies* 21 (1990): 139-52.

This is O'Connell's response to Van Fleteren's "A Reply to Robert O'Connell" (**228**), which presumably ends their public debate. *See also*: **212, 228**.

217 O'Meara, John. "Augustine and Neo-Platonism." *Recherches Augustiniennes* 1 (1958): 91-111.

O'Meara reviews the history of the *libri platonicorum* problem (that is, the problem concerning which Neoplatonic authors Augustine was influenced by). He makes a case for the influence of both Plotinus and Porphyry, then invites the reader to read the *Confessions* (7.13-8.30) and judge for herself.

218 O'Meara, John. "The Neoplatonism of Saint Augustine." In *Neoplatonism and Christian Thought*, ed. by Dominic O'Meara, 34-41. Albany, NY: State University of New York Press, 1982.

O'Meara provides an excellent brief review of *Confessions* scholarship since 1888. Then, as before (**217**), he focuses upon the *libri platonicorum* problem. His point is that Augustine was probably influenced by both Plotinus and Porphyry in many subtle ways.

219 O'Meara, John. "Plotinus and Augustine: Exegesis of *Contra Academicos* II, 5." *Revue internationale de philosophie* 24 (1970): 321-37.

O'Meara compares passages from *Confessions* VIII and *Contra Academicos* II, arguing that some of Augustine's apparently Neoplatonic expressions are due to biblical more than Plotinian influences.

220 O'Meara, John. *Porphyry's Philosophy from Oracles in Augustine*. Paris: Études Augustiniennes, 1959.

O'Meara studies Book X of the *City of God* in order to reconstruct Porphyry's lost book, *Philosophy from Oracles*. In an appendix (or corollary), he demonstrates the presence of Porphyry's text in the *Confessions* and other works by Augustine.

221   Rist, John. "A Man of Monstrous Vanity." *Journal of Theological Studies* 42 (April 1991): 138-43.

In Book VII of the *Confessions*, Augustine tells how he received some translated books of Platonist philosophers from a "man of monstrous vanity." Who was this intermediary? Rist reviews the literature on this question, then proposes that Praetextatus is the most likely person.

222   Starnes, Colin. "Saint Augustine and the Vision of the Truth: A Commentary on the Seventh Book of Augustine's *Confessions*." *Dionysius* 1 (December 1977): 85-126.

Starnes's commentary is well conceived and interesting. He explains how Augustine lost faith with Manicheism, turned to scepticism only to be disillusioned again, then finally came to appreciate the inner quest for truth (the topic of Book VII) upon discovering the Neoplatonists.

223   Torchia, N. Joseph. "'*Pondus meum amor meus*': The Weight-Metaphor in Augustine's Early Philosophy." *Augustinian Studies* 21 (1990): 163-76.

Pondus, the physical metaphor for "weight," plays an important role in Augustine's theory of the soul's fall, which he adapted from classical Greek philosophy. Torchia investigates the significance of *pondus* in Augustine's early philosophical writings and the *Confessions*. While Augustine may have borrowed from Aristotle and Plotinus, according to Torchia he dealt with different problems (moral freedom, for example).

224   Torchia, N. Joseph. "St. Augustine's Treatment of *superbia* and its Plotinian Affinities." *Augustinian Studies* 18 (1987): 66-80.

Superbia (pride) is the root of Augustine's moral triad of vices (*see also*: **383**). Relying upon the *Confessions* and Augustine's early philosophical writings, Torchia investigates the kinship between *superbia* and Plotinus's concept of *tolma*. Both represent root faults, apostasy, idolotry, and temporality.

225   Van Fleteren, Frederick. "Augustine's Ascent of the Soul in Book VII of the *Confessions*: A Reconsideration." *Augustinian Studies* 5 (1974): 29-72.

Van Fleteren provides detailed analysis of Augustine's attempted vision of God at Milan as recorded in *Confessions* Book VII. Then he compares the *Confessions* text with similar ascensional movements in the Cassiciacum dialogues. Apparently, Augustine tried to sustain a mystical vision for some years after his conversion.

226   Van Fleteren, Frederick. "The Early Works of Augustine and His Ascents at Milan." *Studies in Medieval Culture* 10 (1977): 19-23.
Van Fleteren argues that aspiration to the vision of God is the ruling motif of Augustine's writings until 391 AD. The intellectual ascents at Milan, described in Book VII of the *Confessions*, were failed attempts to achieve that vision. As time passed, Augustine's interpretation of ascent became less idealized and philosophical.

227   Van Fleteren, Frederick. "*Per Speculum et in aenigmate*: 1 Corinthians 13:12 in the Writings of St. Augustine." *Augustinian Studies* 23 (1992): 69-102.

Van Fleteren challenges O'Connell's view that Augustine's use of a Corinthians passage in Book VIII of the *Confessions* implies that the "mystical" experience mentioned in Book VII is not mystical (**216**). Van Fleteren concludes that his prior position (that Augustine had a fleeting glimpse of the divine in Milan) is still correct. He is convinced that this mystical ascent of the soul (not its fall, as O'Connell argues) forms the central motif of Augustine's early works. *See also*: **214-15**.

228   Van Fleteren, Frederick. "A Reply to Robert O'Connell." *Augustinian Studies* 21 (1990): 127-37.

Van Fleteren defends his earlier published writings (**225, 226**) against O'Connell's criticisms concerning which Neoplatonic writings Augustine read at Milan (**212**). O'Connell thinks Augustine read only Plotinus, Van Fleteren that he read Porphyry as well. Van Fleteren criticises O'Connell for over-emphasizing the influence of Plotinus's fallen soul doctrine in Augustine's thought. *See also*: **216**.

229   Zum Brunn, Emilie. *St. Augustine: Being and Nothingness*. Trans. by Ruth Namad. New York: Paragon House, 1988.

Zum Brunn interprets the earlier works of Augustine, particularly the *Confessions*, in order to explain his spiritual ontology. She does not think that Christianity significantly distinguishes Augustine's thought from other Platonists.

SELF-CONCEPTION

See also: **015-16, 022-23, 026, 037-40, 042-45, 058-60, 104, 124, 130, 135, 194, 215, 274, 280, 285, 303, 408**

230   Goff, Robert. "The Language of Self-Transformation in Plato and Augustine." *Man and World: An International Philosophical Review* 4 (November 1971): 413-35.

Goff argues that Plato's *Meno* and Books X and XI of the *Confessions* both concern similar problems with language and self-identity. At the beginning of each text there are unanswerable questions which lead to doubt about the act of questioning itself. Futility and groundlessness are experienced, then a new direction (self-transformation) is found which invites the reader to do likewise.

231 Hundert, E. "Augustine and the Sources of the Divided Self." *Political Theory: An International Journal of Political Philosophy* 20 (February 1992): 86-104.

Relying upon Augustine's *Confessions* and *City of God*, Hundert attempts to correct Charles Taylor's discussion of Augustine in *Sources of the Self* (Harvard, 1989). Taylor ignores Augustine's strategies for portrayal of evil, pride, and self-suspicion, which leads him to entertain a more optimistic view of the Augustinian legacy of self-understanding than is warranted.

232 Powers, Patrick. *The Concept of Guilt in the Confessions of St. Augustine: A Phenomenological Study*. Pittsburg, PA: Duquesne University, 1978.

Ph.D. dissertation. Powers provides philosophical analysis of guilt in order to understand its role in striving for self completion. Guilt discloses self-identity, but also conceals it.

233 Ramirez, J. Roland. "Augustine's Numbering Numbers and the Immortality of the Human Soul." *Augustinian Studies* 21 (1990): 153-61.

In Book X of the *Confessions* Augustine makes a distinction between numbered numbers and numbering numbers. Ramirez explains the significance of this distinction for Augustine's understanding of the immortal soul.

TIME AND ETERNITY

See also: **014, 025, 042, 107, 125, 186, 206, 208, 224, 269, 275, 344, 392, 415, 420**

234 Barton, W. B. "Time and Language: Another Look at St. Augustine's Question." *Southern Journal of Philosophy* 5 (Fall 1967): 200-05.

Barton defends Augustine's question about the nature of time against the tendency by analytic philosophers (following Wittgenstein, **272-73**) to assume he has misunderstood the purpose of the word "time." He appeals chiefly to Husserl in his defense (**245**).

235 Bertman, Martin. "Augustine on Time, With Reference to Kant." *The Journal of Value Inquiry* 20 (1986): 223-34.

Humans are like God in some ways, not so in others; Augustine's discussion of time in Book XI employs both stances according to Bertman. He sorts out the complexities and refers to Kant in order to make Augustine's existential theory of time understandable to the modern reader.

236   Callahan, John. *Four Views of Time in Ancient Philosophy*. Cambridge, MA: Harvard University Press, 1948.

Callahan presents the views of time in Plato's *Timaeus*, Aristotle's *Physics*, Plotinus's *Enneads*, and Augustine's *Confessions*. He emphasizes the uniqueness of each thinker's approach, and claims that most modern thinking about time is traceable to one of these four. What is unique about Augustine's view of time is his psychological approach.

237   Callahan, John. "Basil of Caesarea: A New Source for St. Augustine's Theory of Time." In *Harvard Studies in Classical Philology, 63*, anonymously edited, 437-54. Cambridge, MA: Harvard University Press, 1958.

Callahan argues that chapter 23 of Book XI of the *Confessions* is borrowed from Basil, which means that Augustine's psychological theory of time, particularly his concept of the distended soul, is not of Plotinian derivation as commonly believed. *See also*: **268**.

238   Caranfa, Angelo. "Augustine and Proust on Time." *History of European Ideas* 7 (1986): 161-74.

Caranfa claims both Augustine and Proust share the view that public time is inadequate for understanding the inner life. Both have different views of what vocation the inner life is for, yet they share a common sense of human pilgrimage.

239   Cavadini, John. "Time and Ascent in *Confessions* XI." In *Collectanea Augustiniana: Augustine Presbyter Factus Sum*, ed. by Joseph Lienhard, Earl Muller, and Roland Teske, 171-85. New York: Peter Lang, 1993.

Cavadini thinks that Augustine is more concerned with our awareness of time than with the question of time's nature. Awareness of time, for Augustine, is coincidently an awareness about God. Hence Cavadini claims that Augustine is describing an ascent of the soul rather than writing a treatise on time.

240   Doss, Seale. "Copernicus Revisited: Time Versus 'Time' Versus Time." *Philosophy and Phenomenological Research: A Quarterly Journal* 31 (December 1970): 193-211.

Doss analyzes what Wittgenstein called the Augustinian puzzle concerning time: we measure time, yet we cannot measure it (**272-73**). The puzzle stems from an unrealistic expectation of language (that the word "time" ought to imply more than its usage allows). The reference to Copernicus indicates Doss's belief that Wittgenstein's grammatical interpretation of time furthers Kant's transcendental philosophy (Kant's Copernican revolution). *See also*: **241, 250, 265**.

241   Findlay, J. N. "Time: A Treatment of Some Puzzles." In *The Philosophy of Time: A Collection of Essays*, ed. by Richard Gale, 143-62. New Jersey: Humanities Press, 1978.

Inspired by Wittgenstein (**272-73**), Findlay investigates various perplexities concerning time, and suggests ways to circumvent them. One perplexity (or set of perplexities) he analyzes stems from Augustine's *Confessions*: how something can have temporal duration if future and past do not exist. *See also*: **240, 250, 265**.

242   Gay, David. "The Circumscription of Time in *Samson Agonistes*." *Christianity and Literature* 42 (Winter 1993): 261-78.

Gay argues that Milton's poem about Samson is not unduly critical of biblical tradition as at least one recent interpreter claims. Gay employs a notion of "Augustinian temporality," derived from the *Confessions*, to make his point.

243   Hausheer, Herman. "St. Augustine's Conception of Time." *The Philosophical Review* 46 (1937): 503-12.

Hausheer offers a careful review of Augustine's theory of time in Book XI of the *Confessions*. Then he resolves several problems that Augustine never addressed, such as the individual variability of the experience of the present. He concludes that Augustine was the first person to discover the meaning of time, despite the fact that Plato, Aristotle, and Plotinus had written about time previously.

244   Huddlestun, Bernard. "St. Augustine and Aristotle on Time and History." In *Heirs and Ancestors*, ed. by John Ryan, 279-91. Studies in Philosophy and the History of Philosophy, 6. Washington: Catholic University of America Press, 1973.

Huddlestun challenges the common view that Aristotle's view of history (or humanly significant time) was circular while Augustine's was not. He employs Aristotle's ethical distinction between theory and practice to demonstrate that Aristotle, more than Augustine, appreciated the ephemeral actions of individuals and political communities (which, in modern times, we would call history).

245   Husserl, Edmund. *The Phenomenology of Internal Time-Consciousness*. Trans. by James Churchill. Bloomington, IN: Indiana University Press, 1964.

Husserl does not interpret the *Confessions* as such in this lecture book, though he begins with high praise of Augustine's earlier analysis of time. Husserl's work confirms the validity of Augustine's theory of time by extending it further. *See*: **234**.

246   Johnson, John. *The Significance of the Plotinian Fallen-Soul Doctrine for an Interpretation of the Unitary Character of Augustine's View of Time*. St. Louis: St. Louis University, 1982.

Ph.D. dissertation. In the *Confessions*, Augustine says that time and humanity were created together; in the *City of God*, he intimates that time was created first. Johnson refers to Plotinus's fallen soul doctrine in order to reconcile the apparent discrepancy between these two different conceptions of time in Augustine's work.

247   Jordan, Robert. "Time and Contingency in St. Augustine." *Review of Metaphysics* 8 (March 1955): 394-417.

Jordan employs a passage from the *City of God* to explain why Augustine bothered to investigate the nature of time (in the *Confessions*) in the first place. He claims that Augustine's interest in time is moral rather than cosmological. Augustine investigates the limitations of contingent, finite being.

248   Kirwan, Christopher. *Augustine*. The Arguments of the Philosophers. New York: Routledge, 1989.

Kirwan writes about Augustine's philosophy, focusing primarily on the issues of free will and time. He analyzes the *Confessions* in two chapters devoted to the discussion of time. Of particular interest to Kirwan is Augustine's solution to the problem of time's beginning.

249   Lacey, Hugh. "Empiricism and Augustine's Problems about Time." *Review of Metaphysics* 22 (December 1968): 219-45.

Lacey believes that Augustine's discussion of time in the *Confessions* revolves around two traditional problems in the metaphysics of time: objectivity versus subjectivity, and absolute versus relational. He compares Augustine's subjective theory of time to Reichenbach's causal theory, which results in insight about what an empirically verifiable understanding of time would entail.

250   McEvoy, James. "St. Augustine's Account of Time and Wittgenstein's Criticisms." *Review of Metaphysics* 37 (March 1984): 547-78.

With caution and admiration, McEvoy presents Augustine's argument concerning time in Book XI for critical evaluation (and defense) in light of

Wittgenstein's misgivings (272-73): that Augustine attempts to establish a scientific language for a philosophical problem; that Augustine confuses the measurement of time with the measurement of space; that Augustine seems to think we have a measuring clock in our minds; and that Augustine never explains what time is. See also: 240, 241, 265.

251 Merleau-Ponty, J. "Ideas of Beginnings and Endings in Cosmology." In The Study of Time, ed. by N. Lawrence, 330-50. New York: Springer, 1978.

Merleau-Ponty thinks that the passage of time has had little effect on the philosophy of time. He means that twentieth century cosmology still works within ancient categories concerning the nature of time and the beginning of the cosmos. Augustine's theory of time is discussed as a variant of Plato's, which is one of three Greek options. Merleau-Ponty claims that Democritus's view prevails today (infinite space and time, no final causality, no cosmic beginning).

252 Morrison, John. "Augustine's Two Theories of Time." The New Scholasticism 45 (Autumn 1971): 600-10.

Morrison claims that Augustine's view of time in the Confessions differs from his view of time in the City of God. In the former, time is viewed as subjective in nature, coming to be with the soul. In the latter, time is viewed as preceeding human creation. Furthermore, Morrison claims that Augustine's philosophy of history in the City of God presupposes a theory of time consistent only with the Confessions. He resolves the apparent inconsistency by referring to Augustine's view of angels, which also have a stake in history. See also: 270.

253 Mundle, C. W. "Augustine's Pervasive Error Concerning Time." Philosophy 41 (1966): 165-68.

Mundle wonders why philosophers accept Augustine's problematic understanding of present time (the present does not endure) instead of realizing that our awareness of time's flow is nothing but an awareness of things changing.

254 Niarchos, C. G. "Aristotelian and Plotinian Influences on St. Augustine's Views of Time." Philosophia 15-16 (1985-86): 332-51.

Niarchos analyzes Aristotle's conception of time, and Plotinus's. Then he demonstrates the influence of these philosophers upon Augustine's speculations about time. He concludes that Christianity helped Augustine to understand time in a more penetrating fashion.

255 O'Daly, Gerard. "Augustine on the Measurement of Time: Some Comparisons With Aristotelian and Stoic Texts." In NeoPlatonism and Early Christian Thought: Essays in Honour of A. H. Armstrong, ed. by H. Blumenthal and Robert Markus, 171-79. London: Variorum Publications, 1981.

O'Daly compares Augustine's question about how to measure time (*Confessions,* Book XI) with Aristotle's *de memoria* and certain Stoic fragments. He concludes that Augustine may have been aware of these sources since his arguments address traditional problems.

256   Polk, Danne. "Temporal Impermanence and the Disparity of Time and Eternity." *Augustinian Studies* 22 (1991): 63-82.

Polk compares Augustine's discussion of time and eternity in Book XI of the *Confessions* to Husserl's discussion of time and memory in *Phenomenology of Internal Time-Consciousness* (**245**).

257   Quinn, John. "The Concept of Time in St. Augustine." *Augustinianum* 5 (February 1965): 5-57.

Quinn presents Augustine's discussion of time from the *Confessions* as a theory still relevant in the age of science. He breaks down Augustine's text into a three stage dialectic, and briefly compares Augustine's understanding of time with Bergson's and Aristotle's.

258   Rau, Catherine. "Theories of Time in Ancient Philosophy." *The Philosophical Review* 62 (1953): 514-25.

Rau discusses Plotinus's attempt to develop Plato's theory of time while discrediting Aristotle's theory. Then she compares Plotinus's theory to Augustine's, claiming that Augustine provides the most advanced theory of time in ancient philosophy (even anticipating Kant and relativity).

259   Ravicz, Marilyn. "St. Augustine: Time and Eternity." *Thomist* 22 (October 1959): 542-54.

Ravicz explores the ontological implications of Augustine's understanding of time and eternity, focusing on the relation of the unchangeable to the changeable, being to nonbeing, and salvation to history. Her point is to demonstrate the uniquely Christian and theological basis for Augustine's thought.

260   Ricoeur, Paul. *Time and Narrative* 3 vols. Trans. by Kathy Blamey and David Pellauer. Chicago: University of Chicago Press, 1984-88.

Ricoeur pairs Augustine's discussion of time in the *Confessions* with Aristotle's discussion of plot in the *Poetics*, claiming that time, like life, must be understood as a narrative that weaves together psychological and cosmological interpretations. He demonstrates how Husserl and Heidegger made the same mistakes as Augustine, trying to explain time as a phenomenon of the inner self alone.

261 Ross, Donald. "Time, the Heaven of Heavens, and Memory in Augustine's *Confessions*." *Augustinian Studies* 22 (1991): 191-205.

Ross addresses the problem of apparent inconsistency in Augustine's two-part discussion of time in Book XI of the *Confessions*. In a first part (1.1-13.16), Augustine's response to Manichean criticism of the Christian doctrine of creation, time is thought to be something real in the physical universe. However, in a second part (14.17-31.41) Augustine concludes that time is merely an extension of the mind. Ross argues that time is real for Augustine, but its sequentialization is mind-dependent.

262 Severson, Richard. *Time, Death, and Eternity: Reflecting on Augustine's Confessions in Light of Heidegger's Being and Time*. American Theological Library Association Monograph Series, 36. Lanham, MD: Scarecrow Press, 1995.

Based on a Ph.D. dissertation, University of Iowa. Severson follows Ricoeur's comparison of Augustine and Heidegger (**260**) to its theological conclusions. He claims that Heidegger gives death too much significance, overlooking the meaning of religious categories such as eternity that transcend death's ultimacy.

263 Smith, Pamela. "Augustinian Time." *American Benedictine Review* 29 (December 1978): 371-80.

Smith claims that Augustine's introspection teaches the same lessons about time as Einstein's science.

264 Sorabji, Richard. *Time, Creation and the Continuum: Theories in Antiquity and the Early Middle Ages*. Ithaca, NY: Cornell University Press, 1983.

Sorabji reviews Greek philosophical thought about time up to and including developments in Christian and Islamic theology. His approach is thematic, first exploring the question of time's reality, then time and eternity, time and creation, creation and cause, and finally time-atoms and the continuum. Sorabji discusses the *Confessions* extensively in the sections on the reality of time and time and eternity. In the latter section, he distinguishes Augustine's sense of mysticism from Plotinus's, which adds insight to the Neoplatonism debate in *Confessions* scholarship.

265 Suter, Ronald. "Augustine on Time With Some Criticisms from Wittgenstein." *Revue internationale de philosophie* 61-62 (1962): 378-94.

Suter presents Augustine's explanation of time from the *Confessions*, reviews Wittgenstein's grammatical criticisms (**272-73**), then concludes that Augustine's explanation is too primitive. *See also*: **240, 241, 250**.

266   Teske, Roland. "The World-Soul and Time in St. Augustine."
Augustinian Studies 14 (1983): 75-92.
Teske examines some of Augustine's early writings in order to demonstrate that
he held a Plotinian doctrine of world-soul with which individual souls are
identical. Then he demonstrates how this doctrine influenced Augustine's
discussion of heaven and hell and time in the *Confessions*.

267   Thompson, Christopher. "The Theological Dimension of Time in
Confessiones XI." In *Collectanea Augustiniana: Augustine Presbyter Factus
Sum*, ed. by Joseph Lienhard, Earl Muller, and Roland Teske, 187-93. New
York: Peter Lang, 1993.

Thompson claims that Augustine's theory of time is theological rather than
psychological. Those who characterize it as psychological tend to ignore the
context of Book XI, in which Augustine situates the doctrine of creation within
the doctrine of Word.

268   Tzamalikos, P. "Origen: The Source of Augustine's Theory of Time."
Philosophia 17-18 (1987-88): 396-418.

Tzamalikos provides a detailed discussion of Origen's conception of time,
distinguishing it from Stoicism and Neoplatonism. Then he demonstrates how
Augustine's theory of time relies upon Origen's. He criticises Callahan (**237**) for
claiming that Basil was the source of Augustine's theory. According to
Tzamalikos, Basil borrowed his ideas about time from Origen.

269   Vance, Eugene. "Saint Augustine: Language as Temporality." In
Mimesis: From Mirror to Method, Augustine to Descartes, ed. by John Lyons
and S. Nichols, 20-35. Hanover, NH: University Press of New England, 1982.

Augustine's theory of time in the *Confessions* is based upon observations of a
speech event. Vance explains how Augustine's theory of language or signs
derives from his understanding of time; language is limited in the same manner
as time, and for the same reasons. Both fall short in comparison to the divine.

270   Von Jess, Wilma. "Augustine: A Consistent and Unitary Theory of Time."
The New Scholasticism 46 (Summer 1972): 337-51.

Von Jess responds to Morrison's article (**252**), claiming that he misrepresents
Augustine's thought on at least two critical points. First, Augustine's view of
time in the *Confessions* is not purely subjective as Morrison claims. Second, he
misunderstands the relation between angels and history.

271   Von Jess, Wilma. "Divine Eternity in the Doctrine of St. Augustine."
Augustinian Studies 6 (1975): 75-96.

Von Jess explains Augustine's solutions to various problems that naturally occur when speaking about God's nature. Her claim is that Augustine relies upon both affirmative and negative statements in order to preserve the paradox of eternity. She refers to the *Confessions* and other texts of Augustine's.

272 Wittgenstein, Ludwig. *The Blue and Brown Books.* Oxford: Basil Blackwell, 1958.

In the *Blue Book*, a preparatory notebook for *Philosophical Investigations* (**273**), Wittgenstein discusses several problems with Augustine's theory of time: Augustine thinks there is a measuring clock in the mind, confuses time with space, and never explains what time really is.

273 Wittgenstein, Ludwig. *Philosophical Investigations.* Trans. by G. E. M. Anscombe. New York: Macmillan, 1953.

As he did in the *Blue Book* (**272**), Wittgenstein once again briefly criticises Augustine's discussion of time. In this philosophical classic, he faults Augustine for misunderstanding the role of logic in philosophy as opposed to science. Wittgenstein's remarks inspired others to explore Augustine's theory of time. *See also*: **240-41, 250, 265.**

6

Psychological Criticism

AUGUSTINE AS MODEL THERAPIST

See also: **195**

274 Niño, Andrés. "Restoration of the Self: A Therapeutic Paradigm from Augustine's *Confessions*." *Psychotherapy* 27 (Spring 1990): 8-18.

Niño claims that the *Confessions* can serve as a therapeutic model for dealing with fragmentation of the self. He extracts five elements of self restoration from Augustine's text: recognition of self-fragmentation, return to interiority, recollection in dialogue with God, movement beyond the boundaries of self, and creative responses in continuity.

275 Versfeld, Martin. "St. Augustine as Psychotherapist." *Blackfriars* 45 (March 1964): 98-110.

Because they never separated problems of morals, politics, and mental health, Versfeld thinks Plato and Augustine are the greatest psychotherapists. He relies primarily upon the *Confessions*, the *City of God*, and *de trinitate* in presenting Augustine's anthropology, the key concepts of which are time and love. Versfeld claims that Augustine's therapeutic message is that we should enjoy being in the time we have.

CHILDHOOD

See also: **281-82, 287, 308, 339, 357, 375, 446-47, 451, 457**

276 Dombrowski, Daniel. "Starnes on Augustine's Theory of Infancy: A Piagetian Critique." *Augustinian Studies* 11 (1980): 125-33.

Relying upon Piaget's developmental understanding of consciousness and rationality, Dombrowski criticizes Augustine's intellectual interpretation of infancy (and he criticizes Starnes [381] to the extent that he agrees with Augustine). The problem is that Augustine thinks that rationality is preformed or pregiven instead of being gradually acquired. Dombrowski concludes with a critique of Augustine's notion of original sin.

277   Ferrari, Leo. "The Boyhood Beatings of Augustine." *Augustinian Studies* 5 (1974): 1-14.

Ferrari claims that Augustine's proclivity for sadness and self-reproach is a result of boyhood beatings described in the *Confessions*. He claims that Augustine's stern picture of God is a further consequence of beatings at the hands of his teachers.

278   Hopkins, Brooke. "St. Augustine's *Confessions*: The Pear-Stealing Episode." *American Imago: A Psychoanalytic Journal for Culture, Science and the Arts* 38 (Spring 1981): 97-104.

Hopkins interprets Augustine's pear-stealing episode from the point of view of Winnicott's theory that some childhood acts of stealing are motivated by a search for one's mother.

FREUDIAN PSYCHOANALYSIS

See also: **097, 286-87, 294, 296, 305, 313**

279   Browning, Don. "The Psychoanalytic Interpretation of St. Augustine's *Confessions*: An Assessment and New Probe." In *Psychoanalysis and Religion*, ed. by Joseph Smith and Susan Handelman, 136-59. Psychiatry and the Humanities, 11. Baltimore: Johns Hopkins University Press, 1990.

In this review essay Browning discusses four problems with psychoanalytic interpretations of the *Confessions* (**059, 128, 281-84, 286-87, 294, 298, 300, 303, 431**) . First, there is insufficient attention to the autobiographical genre; second, there is no attempt to combine the insights of Oedipal and narcissistic interpretation; third, there is no attempt to contribute to the theory of psychoanalytic interpretation; and fourth, they have not investigated the psychology of religion enterprise. He makes a helpful distinction between early psychoanalytic interpretations (mainly done by psychologists and psychiatrists) and more recent ones (mainly done by humanistic scholars).

280   Earl, James. "Preface: Augustine, Freud, Lacan." *Thought: A Review of Culture and Idea* 61 (March 1986): 7-15.

Earl writes the initial, prefatory article in a special issue devoted to postmodern perspectives of psychoanalysis and religion. He articulates Augustine's theory of the Inner Master (or voice of Christ), which is derived from his self-analysis in the *Confessions*. Earl then asks how this theory can inform our understanding of Freud's "trinity," and Lacan's.

281 Kligerman, Charles. "A Psychoanalytic Study of the *Confessions* of St. Augustine." *Journal of the American Psychoanalytic Association* 5 (July 1957): 469-84.

This is a Freudian study of the *Confessions*, pointing out Augustine's pre-Oedipal anxieties and unresolved Oedipal conflicts. Kligerman is especially interested in Augustine's boyhood fascination with Virgil's story of Aeneas and Dido, which is compulsively repeated by Augustine when he leaves Carthage (and his mother) for Rome.

282 Rigby, Paul. "Paul Ricoeur, Freudianism, and Augustine's *Confessions*." *Journal of the American Academy of Religion* 53 (March 1985): 93-114.

Rigby provides a Freudian reading of the *Confessions* that challenges other Freudian interpreters who claim Augustine could not resolve his Oedipal conflicts in the appropriate way. Instead, Rigby claims that the conversion of Patricius played a more critical role in Augustine's self-understanding than did childhood competition for Monica's affections.

283 Woollcott, Philip. "Some Considerations of Creativity and Religious Experience in St. Augustine of Hippo." *Journal for the Scientific Study of Religion* 5 (Spring 1966): 273-83.

Woollcott psychoanalyzes Augustine, based on the *Confessions*, focusing particularly upon his creative abilities to resolve conflicts both for himself and his times. Oedipal conflict is emphasized.

NARCISSISM

See also: **080, 279, 294, 296**

284 Bakan, David. "Some Thoughts on Reading Augustine's *Confessions*." *Journal for the Scientific Study of Religion* 5 (October 1965): 149-52.

Bakan thinks Augustine is disingenuous and narcissistic in his confessional self-reproach, which covers up a perverse power struggle with God.

285 Beers, William. "The *Confessions* of Augustine: Narcissistic Elements." *American Imago: A Psychoanalytic Journal for Culture, Science and the Arts* 45 (Spring 1988): 107-25.

Beers employs Kohut's narcissistic theory in reading the *Confessions*. He claims that Augustine never achieved cohesive adult selfhood because of lingering narcissistic problems pertaining chiefly to his relationship with Monica. These lingering problems determine Augustine's religious thought, according to Beers, including the metaphorical forms of the *Confessions*.

286   Capps, Donald. "Augustine as Narcissist: Comments on Paul Rigby's 'Paul Ricoeur, Freudianism, and Augustine's *Confessions*'." *Journal of the American Academy of Religion* 53 (March 1985): 116-27.

Capps argues that Oedipal readings of the *Confessions*, Rigby's in particular (**282**), overlook the more important issue of Augustine's inability to love. Commenting on Rigby's article, he outlines what a narcissistic reading of Augustine's text would look like.

287   Gay, Volney. "Augustine: The Reader as Selfobject." *Journal for the Scientific Study of Religion* 25 (March 1986): 64-76.

Gay reads the *Confessions* as an ambiguous attempt to make God and his readers "selfobjects," that is, stabilizing influences who will affirm Augustine's narcissistic need to believe that his life is unique and worth living. This plea for selfobject relationships is ambiguous because Augustine, like Freud, thinks that the mature adult should outgrow childhood needs.

NON-FREUDIAN ANALYSIS

See also: **276-78, 292, 305**

288   Capps, Donald. "An Allportian Analysis of Augustine." *International Journal for the Psychology of Religion* 4 (1994): 205-28.

Psychology of religion includes two prominent schools of thought, Freudian and Allportian. Capps tries to lessen the gap between them by offering this (the first) Allportian interpretation of Augustine's *Confessions*. He focuses upon the first nine books only, identifying eight major character traits. Augustine's most important trait was intellectual problem solver, the most problematic was personal shame.

289   Elledge, W. "Embracing Augustine: Reach, Restraint, and Romantic Resolution in the *Confessions*." *Journal for the Scientific Study of Religion* 27 (March 1988): 72-89.

Elledge reads Augustine's conversion as a psychological healing of previous vexed relationships, particularly with Monica and his unnamed friend who died. This article is a review essay of sorts for psychological literature on the *Confessions*.

290   Pruyser, Paul. "Psychological Examination: Augustine." *Journal for the Scientific Study of Religion* 5 (Spring 1966): 284-89.

Pruyser gives a brief, matter of fact psychological report about Augustine's personality based upon a reading of the *Confessions*.

PSYCHOHISTORY

See also: **027, 128**

291   Archambault, Paul. "Augustine's *Confessiones*: On the Uses and the Limits of Psychobiograpy." In *Collectanea Augustiniana: Augustine: Second Founder of the Faith*, ed. by Joseph Schnaubelt and Frederick Van Fleteren, 83-99. New York: Peter Lang, 1990.

Psychobiographers of Augustine have asserted the following: that he was a tired man when he wrote the *Confessions*; that he wanted to satisfy the secret wishes of a pious mother; that he needed to get away from his possessive mother; that he was secretly homosexual. Archambault wonders whether such insights are helpful for the historian. He thinks that they are, partially, though psychoanalytic language can never be expected to capture the complete sense of religious experience.

292   Byrnes, Joseph. "Historical Interpretation of Augustine: The Promise of James, Allport, and Capps." *International Journal for the Psychology of Religion* 4 (1994): 229-33.

Byrnes believes that Capps's psychological interpretation of the *Confessions* (**288**) is helpful to the historian because it employs the jargon free language of James (**303**) and Allport.

293   Daly, Lawrence. "Psychohistory and St. Augustine's Conversion Process." *Augustiniana* 28 (1978): 231-54.

Daly analyzes how several historians interpret Augustine's conversion in order to illustrate the absence of psychological insight in the ordinary study of history. He recommends psychohistorical analysis so that Augustine's personality will be studied in a more fruitful and straightforward fashion. Includes a review of previous psychological interpretations of Augustine.

294   Fredriksen, Paula. "Augustine and His Analysts: The Possibility of a Psychohistory." *Soundings: An Interdisciplinary Journal* 61 (Summer 1978): 206-27.

Fredriksen reviews psychoanalytic interpretations of Augustine that focus exclusively on the *Confessions* (**281, 283-84, 290, 297-98, 300**), and finds them lacking. Specifically, they make hasty Freudian generalizations that are unwarranted on historical grounds. Fredriksen presents Peter Brown's *Augustine of Hippo* as a more responsible psychobiography (**128**). She concludes that a narcissistic interpretation of Augustine's personality is better than the standard Oedipal interpretation.

295   Jonte-Pace, Diane. "Augustine on the Couch: Psychohistorical (Mis)readings of the *Confessions.*" *Religion* 23 (January 1993): 71-83.

Jonte-Pace explores the limitations of Augustinian psychohistory in this review article which focuses chiefly upon the twenty essays collected in *Hunger of the Heart* (Society for the Scientific Study of Religion, 1990). She compares 20th century Augustinian psychohistory with 19th century quests for the historical Jesus: the former is as confused as the latter, and awaits its Schweitzer. Three problems are especially problematic (the subject of psychohistory, cultural context, and hermeneutics).

296   TeSelle, Eugene. "Augustine as Client and as Theorist." *Journal for the Scientific Study of Religion* 25 (March 1986): 92-101.

TeSelle finds Oedipal and narcissistic readings of the *Confessions* inadequate. He demonstrates that an historically sensitive and theologically informed interpretation of Augustine's relationships is far more illuminating.

PSYCHOLOGY OF RELIGION

See also: **002, 027, 059, 121, 142, 146, 150, 185, 232, 274-77, 279, 285, 288, 291, 293, 296, 352, 361, 454**

297   Clark, Walter. "Depth and Rationality in Augustine's *Confessions.*" *Journal for the Scientific Study of Religion* 5 (October 1965): 144-48.

That modern psychologists find the *Confessions* interesting and worthy of critical analysis is evidence of Augustine's greatness as a thinker and self observer. Reading the *Confessions*, participating emotionally in Augustine's spiritual adventures, is psychological study of the best kind according to Clark.

298   Dittes, James. "Continuities Between the Life and Thought of Augustine." *Journal for the Scientific Study of Religion* 5 (1965): 130-40.

Using the *Confessions* as his primary resource, Dittes offers psychological analysis of Augustine's position on six theological issues. His claim is that themes of submission dominate Augustine's thought.

299   Dittes, James. "Augustine: Search for a Fail-Safe God to Trust." *Journal for the Scientific Study of Religion* 25 (March 1986): 57-63.

Dittes claims that Augustine's understanding of religion is modeled upon the grief he experienced when his best friend died. The religious search is a search for trust that will not fail. Only a God remote from life is fully trustworthy for Augustine.

300 Dodds, Eric. "Augustine's *Confessions*: A Study of Spiritual Maladjustment." *Hibbert Journal* 26 (October 1927-July 1928): 459-73.

Dodds interprets Augustine psychologically (employing James's categories, **303**) in order to inspire ordinary people to read the *Confessions*. He calls Augustine a new Aeneas, the last original Latin master and the first writer of modern romantic prose.

301 Donnelly, Dorothy. "Augustine of Hippo: Psychologist-Saint." *Spiritual Life* 25 (Spring 1979): 13-26.

Donnelly challenges pessimistic psychological readings of the *Confessions*, Dodds's in particular. She claims that Augustine is the best example of a truly religious personality, and she defends his psychological and theological achievements.

302 Havens, Joseph. "Notes on Augustine's *Confessions*." *Journal for the Scientific Study of Religion* 5 (October 1965): 141-43.

Havens contrasts psychological and theological readings of Augustine's description of inner conflict. He sees no way to reconcile the two perspectives.

303 James, William. *The Varieties of Religious Experience: A Study in Human Nature.* New York: New American Library Books, 1958.

In his classic of religious psychology, James very briefly interprets the *Confessions*. He claims that Augustine provides a perfect illustration of the divided self, which is the basis for the twice born character type.

304 Kristo, Jure. *Looking for God in Time and Memory: Psychology, Theology, and Spirituality in Augustine's Confessions.* Lanham, MD: University Press of America, 1991.

How does Augustine's personality affect his thinking? Kristo explores this question from a psychological perspective, augmenting previous analyses with his own midlife psychological analysis of Augustine. Kristo believes Augustine's psychological handicaps inform his theology, but he does not think psychological criticism can destroy the independent merits of theology and spirituality.

SEXUALITY

See also: 060, 101, 291, 389, 443, 448-49, 455

305   Bowers, John. "Augustine as Addict: Sex and Texts in the *Confessions*." *Exemplaria: A Journal of Theory in Medieval and Renaissance Studies* 2 (October 1990): 403-48.

Bowers employs psychoanalytic models of Freud and Jung to interpret Augustine's lifelong spiritual problem as sexual addiction. Secondly, he views Augustine's turn to "texts" (especially Genesis in the later books of the *Confessions*) as a replacement for sex. The move from bad behavior (sex) to good conduct (biblical interpretation) helps explain the structural bifurcation of Augustine's autobiography. Finally, Bowers argues that Augustine's growing intolerance in later years indicates that his addiction recovery was not successful.

306   Brown, Peter. "Augustine and Sexuality." *Colloquy* 46 (1983): 1-13.

Brown contrasts Augustine's early ascetic interpretation of sexuality in the *Confessions* with his later social interpretation in Book XIV of the *City of God*. It is the later interpretation, which views sexuality as the unique symbolic clue to human fallibility and sin, which influenced Western Christianity so profoundly.

307   Ferrari, Leo. "The Barren Field in Augustine's *Confessions*." *Augustinian Studies* 8 (1977): 55-70.

When Augustine was idled from his studies for a year at the age of sixteen, he was overwhelmed with sexual desire, which he interpreted using the metaphor of a barren or neglected field. Ferrari discusses Augustine's use of this image throughout the Confessions.

308   Ferrari, Leo. "The Gustatory Augustin." *Augustiniana* 29 (1979): 304-15.

Augustine's inward struggle with sex has received much attention. Ferrari claims that his struggle with gluttony was more enduring, however, as passages in Book X of the *Confessions* indicate. Ferrari speculates that this could be a legacy of Augustine's Manicheism, or perhaps a persistent attitude from childhood.

309   Hunter, David. "Augustinian Pessimism?: A New Look at Augustine's Teaching on Sex, Marriage and Celibacy." *Augustinian Studies* 25 (1994): 153-77.

Augustine is frequently accused of being the pessimistic source of harmful teachings regarding sex and marriage. Hunter thinks the "pessimism" label stems from too much atttention being paid to the final decade of Augustine's life.

He looks more carefully at Augustine's earlier writings, including the *Confessions*, in order to balance the picture.

310 Jaspers, Karl. *The Great Philosophers: The Foundations*. Ed. by Hannah Arendt, trans. by Ralph Manheim. New York: Harcourt, Brace and World, 1962.

Jaspers writes critical introductions to the lives of Socrates, Buddha, Confucius, Jesus, Plato, Augustine, and Kant. He does not interpret the *Confessions* as such, but characterizes Augustine as inhuman (and unfeeling) based upon apparently sexist remarks about his concubine in the *Confessions*.

311 Markus, Robert. "Augustine's *Confessions* and the Controversy with Julian of Eclanum: Manichaeism Revisited." In *Collectanea Augustiniana:Mélanges T. J. Van Bavel*, ed. by Bernard Bruning, M. Lamberigts, and J. Van Houtem, 913-25.

Markus sheds light upon the conflict between Augustine and Julian about the goodness of human sexuality. Julian believed that sex had to do with reproductive biology; Augustine that it had to do with eroticism. Augustine's "negative" view stems from an insight garnered from Ambrose about the difference between Manichaeism and Catholicism. Manichees were dualists, Catholics argued for the unity of the self. Augustine believed that sexuality as part of God's original creation was good, but as practiced by fallen human beings it contributed to a loss of unity within the self.

312 Nikkel, David. "St. Augustine on the Goodness of Creaturely Existence." *Duke Divinity School Review* 43 (Fall 1978): 181-87.

Relying upon the *Confessions* and *City of God*, Nikkel reviews Augustine's lifelong struggle to affirm the goodness of life despite the pessimistic atmosphere in which he lived. He was least able to affirm creaturely existence concerning sex.

313 O'Connell, Robert. "Sexuality in St. Augustine." In *Augustine Today*, ed. by R. Neuhaus, 60-87. Encounter Series, 16. Grand Rapids, MI: William Eerdmans, 1993.

O'Connell reads passages from the *Confessions* that pertain to sexuality in order to refute psychoanalytic interpretations that defy common sense.

314 O'Meara, John. "Augustine's Attitude to Love in the Context of his Influence on Christian Ethics." *Arethusa* 2 (1969): 46-60.

O'Meara cautions against the convention of thinking that Augustine was a modern man. One consequence is to misunderstand how typically ancient

Augustine was in his attitude toward love and human sexuality. Referring mostly to the *Confessions*, O'Meara puts Augustine's "puritanism" into its proper cultural context. *See also*: **316**.

315 O'Meara, John. "Augustine's Understanding of the Creation and Fall." *Maynooth Review* 10 (1984): 52-62.

O'Meara reflects upon Augustine's view of male and female relations by comparing his interpretations of Genesis from the *Confessions* and *de genesi ad litteram*. He believes that Augustine was especially sympathetic to women, contrary to his reputation.

316 O'Meara, John. "Virgil and Augustine: The Roman Background to Christian Sexuality." *Augustinus* 13 (1968): 307-26.

O'Meara responds to the charge that Augustine is responsible for Christian pessimism regarding sexuality. He disputes some of the charge (not all of it) by tracing the influence of Virgil on Augustine, particularly in the *Confessions* account of his "profligate" youth. Virgil was fascinated by the theme of love, and yet portrayed Aeneas's rejection of love at the bidding of a deity. *See also*: **086-87, 314**.

317 Power, Kim. "*Sed unam tamen*: Augustine and his Concubine." *Augustinian Studies* 23 (1992): 49-76.

Power investigates the psycho-social dynamics of Augustine's relationship with his concubine, briefly mentioned in the *Confessions*. She evaluates his sexuality from the point of view of grief psychology, and reflects on how the concubinage experience was incorporated into his theology.

7

Spirituality and Reader Guidance

DESIRE

See also: 112, 118, 143, 191

318 Babcock, William. "Augustine and the Spirituality of Desire."
Augustinian Studies 25 (1994): 179-99.

Babcock depicts Augustine's understanding of religious life as a spirituality of
desire. He grounds this interpretation in an (anti-Manichean) insight concerning
struggle with competing desires that Augustine shares in Book VIII of the
Confessions.

319 McCarthy, John. "Desire, Recollection and Thought: On Augustine's
Confessions 1,1." *Communio: International Catholic Review* 14 (Summer
1987): 146-57.

McCarthy meditates upon the significance of the *Confessions* for a modern
reader, concluding that Augustine's self-revelation inspires imitation because it
is an icon of God's Word.

320 Miles, Margaret. *Desire and Delight: A New Reading of Augustine's
Confessions*. New York: Crossroad, 1992.

Miles claims that the *Confessions* is a text of pleasure in which Augustine
recounts how he was able to find and keep maximal pleasure by renouncing
worldly desires for spiritual ones. That the *Confessions* is a text of pleasure also
means it is emotionally and intellectually engaging to sensitive readers. Miles
attends to the beauties of Augustine's writing as well as the cultural legacy of his
patriarchal conceptions.

DEVOTIONAL CLASSIC

See also: **100, 102, 145, 297, 300, 319, 368, 382, 445, 452**

321   Allen, Robert. "The *Confessions* of St. Augustine." *National Review* (January 11, 1985): 28 ff.

Allen reflects upon his first encounter with Augustine's *Confessions* as a young man. He thinks the appeal of the book is its hopefulness and presentation of a unique individual.

322   Atkins, Gaius. *Pilgrims of the Lonely Road.* Freeport, NY: Books for Libraries, 1967.

Based upon Lenten lectures delivered prior to 1913, when the first edition of this book was published. Atkins interprets seven spiritual classics, including Augustine's *Confessions*, as quests for peace. He emphasizes the threefold charm of the *Confessions* (spiritual, psychological, and literary masterpiece), and its unique documentation of the birth of a soul.

323   Bowman, Lester. "Saint Augustine: The Restless Human Heart." *The Cord* 16 (September 1966): 273-77.

Bowman discusses the meaning of Christian life today by reflecting upon a famous passage from the *Confessions* about the restlessness of the human heart.

324   Brunhumer, Anne. "The Art of Augustine's *Confessions*." *Thought: A Review of Culture and Idea* 37 (Spring 1962): 109-28.

Brunhumer provides an accounting of the literary quality of the *Confessions* (prayer, odyssey, divine comedy, Everyman's story) which make it a unique classic.

325   Carbine, Francis. "Grace and Gravity in the *Confessions* of Augustine." *Dimension* 9 (Summer 1977): 98-114.

Carbine borrows T. S. Eliot's definition of a classic (a classic embodies catholicity of sensibility), and then demonstrates how the *Confessions* is in particular a classic for our muddled times.

326   Clark, Gillian. *Augustine: The Confessions.* Landmarks of World Literature. New York: Cambridge University Press, 1993.

This is a brief critical introduction to the *Confessions*. Clark provides the necessary background for a thoughtful reading of Augustine's classic. Includes a guide to further reading.

327   Connell, James. *Devotional Classics*. Martha Upton lectures delivered at Manchester College, Oxford. London: Longmans, Green and Company, 1924.

Connell's purpose in this series of lectures is to acquaint future ministers with Christian devotional classics. In the initial lecture, he recounts Augustine's spiritual journey as depicted in the first nine books of the *Confessions*.

328   Corcoran, Gervase. *A Guide to the Confessions of St. Augustine*. Living Flame Series. Dublin: Carmelite Centre of Spirituality, 1981.

Corcoran introduces the nonscholarly reader to the *Confessions* as a classic of Western spirituality. He also proposes a solution to the unity problem, claiming that the three parts of the *Confessions* (Books I-IX, X, XI-XIII) are unified by Augustine's concept of conversion and theory of humanity.

329   Davies, Trevor. *To Live is Christ*. Lectures delivered at the Eaton Memorial Church, Toronto. London: Oxford University Press, 1937.

In twelve lectures Davies discusses books that demonstrate the variety of Christian roads to God. The first lecture is about Augustine's *Confessions*. Davies tries to explain the enduring appeal of Augustine's self-revealing classic.

330   Du Toit, Lionel. "*Confessions* of St. Augustine." *The Expository Times* 69 (March 1958): 164-66.

The *Confessions* is in a league of its own as a devotional classic because of Augustine's intellect according to Du Toit, who reviews some of the reasons why it is still worth reading.

331   Fitch, George. *Comfort Found in Good Old Books*. San Francisco: Paul Elder and Company, 1911.

A collection of articles originally published in the San Francisco *Chronicle*. In his article on the *Confessions*, Fitch attempts to explain why Augustine is still worth reading in a largely scientific age.

332   Knowles, David. "The Catholic Classics, 5: The *Confessions* of St. Augustine." *The Tablet* 175 (May 11, 1940): 456-57.

Knowles reflects upon the unique significance of the *Confessions* as a classic of world literature, particularly its broad genre appeal (theology, spirituality, autobiography, psychology, history).

333   Koley, Robert. "Christian Classic: The *Confessions* of St. Augustine." *Liguorian* 55 (January 1967): 45-6.

Koley claims that Augustine's problems are the same as ours. Like him, we too wonder about evil and the meaning of life. The *Confessions* tells our story of response to God's grace.

334   Laeuchli, Samuel. "What Did Augustine Confess?." *Journal of the American Academy of Religion* 50 (Spring 1982): 379-409.

Laeuchli attempts to re-enact a contemporary version of Augustine's classic through dramatization. His play has four characters, one of whom is Augustine.

335   Lang, Andrew. *Adventures Among Books*. London: Longmans, Green, and Company, 1912.

Lang claims to have written his literary autobiography, in other words, reminiscences of great books he has read. He comments upon major events recorded in the autobiographical part of the *Confessions*, regretting the space Augustine gave to theology. The *Confessions* remind him of the poems of Catullus.

336   Nilson, John. "'Let Me Know You': Augustine's, and Our, Quest for God." *Review for Religious* 37 (July 1978): 533-40.

Nilson demonstrates that the *Confessions* is a classic text in the sense that its message transcends the limits of the times in which it was written. Even today, we can learn the truth about ourselves from Augustine's example according to Nilson.

337   O'Donnell, James. *Augustine*. Boston: Boston University Press, 1984.

O'Donnell intends this book to be an introductory guide to the the major writings of Augustine: *On the Trinity*, *On Christian Doctrine*, *City of God*, and *Confessions*. O'Donnell claims that the *Confessions* is a literary prayer, not an autobiography. Above all, he says, it is a book in which to read about oneself.

338   Pelikan, Jaroslav. *The Mystery of Continuity: Time and History, Memory and Eternity in the Thought of Saint Augustine*. The Richard Lectures for 1984-85, University of Virginia. Charlottesville, VA: University Press of Virginia, 1986.

Focusing on the *Confessions*, *City of God*, and *de trinitate*, Pelikan discusses the deeper continuity that persists through Augustine's more celebrated conversions and discontinuities. For sixteen centuries, the *Confessions* has been the echo of investigations concerning the nature of the self.

339   Robinson, Henry. "Augustine's Pears." *America* 43 (April 19, 1930): 37-38.

Robinson reflects on the history of his own puzzlement concerning the pear
stealing scene in Book II of the *Confessions*. He speculates that it is an example
of pure contrition that has animated Catholic literature through the ages.

340 Russel, Robert. "Man's Search for God in the *Confessions* of Saint
Augustine." In *Second Annual Course on Augustinian Spirituality*, ed. by
Robert Russel, Luc Verheijen, et al., 24-46. Rome: Augustinian Publications,
1976.

Russel reflects on the *Confessions* as an itinerary of the human soul in response
to its maker. He emphasizes the importance of Augustine's text through the
centuries.

341 Starnes, Colin. "*Ad sensum*: A Translation of Augustine's *Confessions*;
Book I." *Dionysius* 11 (December 1987): 63-87.

Starnes provides a loose translation of Book I that attempts to make Augustine's
argument more understandable to modern readers. *See also*: **396**.

342 Thompson, Francis. "The Newman of his Time." In *Literary Criticisms*,
ed. by Terrence Connolly, 16-22. New York: Dutton, 1948.

Thompson, turn of the century British author of *The Hound of Heaven*, wrote
this review of the *Confessions* upon its publication in a new edition. He laments
the custom of publishing only Books I-X, and defends Augustine's classic
against those who would call it dry.

343 Vandenberghe, Bruno. "A Saint for Sinners." *Cross and Crown: A
Thomistic Quarterly of Spiritual Theology* 7 (September 1955): 251-75.

Vandenberghe relies on the *Confessions* and other texts to make the claim that
Augustine is the greatest church father because of his universal appeal. People
are still attracted to Augustine because of his struggles with sin and weakness.

344 Wild, John. "Augustine's *Confessions*." In *Classics of Religious
Devotion*, ed. by Willard Sperry, 3-27. Boston: Beacon Press, 1950.

Wild attends to Augustine's concern with inner religious experience in the
Confessions, evil and time particularly, as a legacy that survived the collapse of
Greco-Roman civilization. He believes that Augustine's inward turn can serve
as a model in our times of societal unrest.

345 Williams, Charles. "Augustine and Athanasius." In *The Image of the City
and Other Essays*, ed. by Anne Ridler, 89-91. London: Oxford University Press,
1958.

In this brief essay, Williams bemoans the tendency of modern readers to focus on inconsequential aspects of the *Confessions*, thus missing the larger (often more difficult) point. Athanasius's *The Incarnation of the Word of God* has faired better in this regard.

FRIENDSHIP

See also: **005, 019, 061, 103, 128, 133, 379, 455**

346   McErlane, Maria. "Friendship According to St. Augustine." *Review for Religious* 41 (July-August 1982): 597-604.

McErlane reflects upon two friends discussed in the *Confessions* (Nebridius and Alypius) and demonstrates how Augustine developed a Christian definition of friendship, that is, friendship rooted in the love of God.

MONICA

See also: **119, 189, 278, 281-82, 285, 289, 291, 361, 363-64, 366, 379**

347   Coyle, J. Kevin. "In Praise of Monica: A Note on the Ostia Experience of *Confessions* IX." *Augustinian Studies* 13 (1982): 87-96.

Coyle claims that the point of Augustine's description of the "mystical" experience at Ostia was to show that Monica had reached the pinnacle of true philosophy, which is to anticipate a deeper union with God after death. Whether Augustine shared her vision or not, and whether either one had a true mystical experience, is beside the point. *See also*: **363-64, 366.**

348   Ferrari, Leo. "Monica on the Wooden Ruler." *Augustinian Studies* 6 (1975): 193-205.

Ferrari explains the moral and symbolic significance of the "wooden ruler" upon which Monica is standing when she dreams that God will save her son from Manicheism. Augustine speaks of this prophetic dream in Book III of the *Confessions*.

349   Ferrari, Leo. "*Christus Via* in Augustine's *Confessions*." *Augustinian Studies* 7 (1976): 47-58.

Ferrari responds to a German study of Monica's dream about a wooden ruler that contradicts his earlier interpretation of that dream (**348**). The German interpreter claims that Christ appears in the dream as the smiling young man. Ferrrari upholds his previous position, that Christ appears as the wooden ruler itself.

350   Ferrari, Leo. "The Dreams of Monica in Augustine's *Confessions*." *Augustinian Studies* 10 (1979): 3-18.

Ferrari analyzes two dreams of Monica that are recorded in the *Confessions*, and one "nondream" that might have been there but is not. He comments upon the role they play in the structure of Augustine's autobiography, concluding that Augustine viewed Monica's dreams as a manifestation of God's will.

351   Gavigan, John. "The Mother of St. Augustine." *American Ecclesiastical Review* 119 (October 1948): 254-80.

Gavigan uses the *Confessions* as a primary source for constructing a portrait of Monica, focusing particularly on the development of her "lovable character." He thinks that Augustine's writings are adequate for an understanding of Monica.

352   Kotila, Heikki. "Monica's Death in Augustine's *Confessions* IX.11-13." In *Studia Patristica* 27, ed. by Elizabeth Livingstone, 337-41. Leuven: Peeters, 1993.

Kotila analyzes Augustine's narrative about the death of Monica as an indication of his pastoral attitude toward prayer for the departed and the cult of the dead. In 392-395 AD, Augustine helped reform popular burial customs in Hippo. His concerns in that effort are reflected in the *Confessions* narrative of Monica's death. In both contexts, Augustine emphasized the eucharist, Christian community, and personal grief.

353   Mierow, Charles. "His Mother's Faith." *The Classical Bulletin* 28 (February 1952): 37-41.

Mierow summarizes the major events narrated in the *Confessions*, focusing upon Augustine's relationship with his mother and her Catholic faith.

354   O'Ferrall, Margaret. "Monica, the Mother of Augustine: A Reconsideration." *Recherches Augustiniennes* 10 (1975): 23-43.

O'Ferrall tries to determine what can be known about Monica in light of two facts: (1) the *Confessions* is virtually our only source of information about Monica; and (2) the historical value of the *Confessions* has been the subject of modern criticism. Despite the problems, several factors about Monica remain clear according to O'Ferrall. We know quite clearly, for example, that she lived a God-centered life which influenced her attitude toward others.

355   O'Meara, John. "Monica, the Mother of Augustine." *The Furrow* 5 (September 1954): 555-62.

What can we know about Monica in light of modern criticism of the *Confessions*, the only historical source about her life? O'Meara reviews the probable record of Monica's life and character, beginning with her Berber heritage.

356   Ryan, W. "Monica's Boy." *Extension* 49 (November 1954): 16 ff.

Ryan reviews the story of Augustine's life as told in the *Confessions* from the point of view of Monica's suffering patience. Her tears and prayers are what saw Augustine through his trials according to Ryan.

357   Spark, Muriel. "St. Monica." *The Month* 17 (May 1957): 309-20.

Spark discusses the character of Monica based upon Augustine's comments about her in the *Confessions*. She contrasts Monica's character before her husband died, and afterwards. Before his death, she was a typical modest, saintly woman; after his death, she became a possessive, meddlesome parent.

MYSTICISM

See also: **216, 225-27, 239, 264, 347, 405, 407, 444, 453**

358   Baird, Marie. "The *Confessions* and the *Cloud of Unknowing*: Longing for God as a Formative and Transformative Experience." *Studies in Formative Spirituality* 11 (February 1990): 73-88.

Baird reads the *Confessions* from the standpoint of Augustine's longing for God understood as a tripartite path of grace (formation, reformation, transformation); then she reads the *Cloud of Unknowing* as the logical fulfillment of Augustine's more personal depiction of the journey to God.

359   Henry, Paul. "Philosophy and Mysticism in the *Confessions* of St. Augustine." *Philosophy Today* 5 (Winter 1961): 242-56.

Henry analyzes two critical experiences in Augustine's path toward Christian conversion. First is his encounter with Neoplatonic philosophy at Milan, which enabled him to resolve intellectual doubts concerning scripture. The second was his mystical experience at Ostia, which enabled him to achieve a state of inner peace. These two aspects of Augustine's religious quest must be seen together according to Henry.

360   Houle, Joseph. "The Mystical Journey and the Garden Archetype in the *Confessions* of St. Augustine." *Studies in Formative Spirituality* 9 (February 1988): 63-77.

Houle argues that the garden archetype appears in the *Confessions* whenever Augustine experiences a transformation of consciousness, that is, whenever he takes another step on the mystical ladder of ascent to God. The garden also represents the structure of reality, the understanding of which is the goal of ascent.

361 Jules-Bois, H. "Vision of Eternal Joy: Plato and the *Confessions* of St. Augustine." *Commonweal* 12 (July 30, 1930): 339-41.

Jules-Bois compares the mystical visions presented in Plato's *Symposium* (conversation between Diotima and Socrates) and Augustine's *Confessions* (conversation between Monica and Augustine at Ostia). The daring of Diotima is contrasted with the humility of Monica. The article concludes with reference to James's definition of religious experience.

362 Kenney, John. "The Presence of Truth in the '*Confessions*'." In *Studia Patristica* 27, ed. by Elizabeth Livingstone, 329-36. Leuven: Peeters, 1993.

Kenney argues against the practice of using a modern understanding of mysticism in order to evaluate Augustine's experience. Instead, he recommends reading the *Confessions* on its own terms, focusing upon Augustine's understanding of contemplation and truth.

363 Mourant, John. "Ostia Reexamined: A Study in the Concept of Mystical Experience." *International Journal for Philosophy of Religion* 1 (Spring 1970): 34-45.

Mourant challenges the view of Henry (**359**), Solignac (**078**), and others that the ecstatic experience Augustine shared with his mother at Ostia, described in Book IX of the *Confessions*, was mystical in the full sense of the term. *See also:* **347**, **364**, **366**.

364 Mourant, John. "A Reply to Dr. von Jess' 'Augustine at Ostia: A Disputed Question'." *Augustinian Studies* 4 (1973): 175-77.

Mourant defends his position that Augustine's experience at Ostia was not fully mystical in the Christian sense (*see:* **347**, **363**, **366**). Only Augustine's conversion (discussed in Book VIII of the *Confessions*) qualifies as genuinely mystical for Mourant.

365 St. Hilaire, George. "The Vision at Ostia: Acquired or Infused?" *The Modern Schoolman* 35 (January 1958): 117-23.

St. Hilaire questions whether the vision at Ostia described in Book IX of the *Confessions* is essentially the same as the intellectual ecstasy at Milan described in Book VII. Making use of the distinction between infused and acquired contemplation, he claims that the Ostia experience was of the infused (i.e., higher mystical) variety.

366   Von Jess, Wilma. "Augustine at Ostia: A Disputed Question." *Augustinian Studies* 4 (1973): 159-74.

Von Jess argues that Mourant was wrong to claim that Augustine's experience at Ostia was not truly mystical (**363**). In one of her fourteen criticisms, she indicates that Mourant neglected the role of grace in Christian mysticism. *See also*: **347, 364**.

ORDINATION

See also: **181, 209, 327**

367   Chadwick, Henry. "On Re-reading the *Confessions*." In *Saint Augustine the Bishop: A Book of Essays*, ed. by F. LeMoine and C. Kleinhenz, 139-60. New York: Garland, 1994.

Chadwick reflects on Augustine's reluctant ordination, noting oblique references to the subject in the *Confessions*. He claims that Augustine practices indirect self-vindication: despising the career in pagan society that he left behind, revering the high calling of the priesthood he entered before writing the *Confessions*.

TEACHING

368   Bainton, Roland. "Saint Augustine's Methods of Religious Teaching." In *The Collected Papers in Church History, Series I: Early and Medieval Christianity*, edited by Roland Bainton, 39-44. Boston: Beacon Press, 1962.

Bainton claims that Augustine's greatest contribution to teaching method was the invention of religious autobiography. He articulates several reasons for the universal appeal of the *Confessions*.

369   Broeniman, Clifford. "The Resurrection of a Latin Classic: The *Confessions* of St. Augustine." *Classical World* 86 (January-February 1993): 209-13.

Broeniman addresses instructors of undergraduate Latin, attempting to convince them to teach the *Confessions*. He says it is easily read by second year students, provides a good introduction to rhetorical tropes and late antiquity, and tells a story that still parallels the lives of young readers.

370   Bubacz, Bruce. "Augustine's Dualism and the Inner-Man." *The Modern Schoolman* 54 (March 1977): 245-57.

Bubacz claims that Augustine's use of the "inner-man" locution is pedagogical, which makes his metaphysical dualism less simplistic and subject to criticism. He compares Augustine's use of inner-man talk to the use of mouse traps and ping-pong balls by physics teachers explaining atomic reactions.

371 Cunningham, Beatrice. "Who are Their Models?" *Religious Teacher's Journal* 27 (October 1993): 38-39.

Cunningham recommends Augustine as a role model for young African Americans.

372 Henninger, Mark. "The Adolescent's Making of Meaning: The Pedagogy of Augustine's *Confessions*." *Journal of Moral Education* 18 (January 1989): 32-34.

Henninger explains why the *Confessions* can foster intellectual and ethical development in students. He employs the research of William Perry concerning the stages that college students pass through: from dualism, to multiplicity, to relativism, to commitment. Henninger demonstrates that Augustine went through these stages, which means that the *Confessions* dramatically portrays the experience of most students today.

373 O'Brien, William. "An Approach to Teaching Augustine's *Confessions*." *Horizons* 5 (Spring 1978): 47-62.

Following Burrell's insight about the experiential rootedness of theological understanding (**431**), O'Brien offers advice about how best to teach the *Confessions*. He believes that teachers should focus upon textual puzzles such as the significance of other stories within the story of Augustine's conversion. Responding to these puzzles, students will learn how Augustine's theology grew out of his life experience.

374 Perreiah, Alan. "St. Augustine's *Confessions*: A Preface to Medieval Philosophy." *Teaching Philosophy* 12 (March 1989): 13-21.

Perreiah asks what recommends the *Confessions* for use in the classroom. His answer: it serves as a good introduction to medieval philosophy, especially epistemology, ethics and metaphysics.

375 Semple, W. H. "Augustinus Rhetor: A Study, From the *Confessions*, of St. Augustine's Secular Career in Education." *Journal of Ecclesiastical History* 1 (July-October 1950): 135-50.

Semple reviews Augustine's educational experience as revealed in the *Confessions*, from the beatings he received as a child to his disillusioned retirement from the teaching profession.

8

Structural Unity of the Text

APPARENT DISUNITY

See also: **183, 305, 342**

376 Sheed, Frank. "St. Augustine: *Confessions*, Books IX-XIII." In *The Great Books: A Christian Appraisal* 4, ed. by H. Gardiner, 49-58. A Symposium on the Fourth Year's Program of the Great Books Foundation. New York: Devin-Adair Company, 1953.

Sheed introduces readers to the "second part" of the *Confessions*, arguing that the last three books in particular are an appendix that demonstrates the profundity of a mind that has found God (the search for whom constitutes the focus of the first part of the *Confessions*, Books I-VIII).

IMPOSED STRUCTURE

See also: **152, 195, 324, 350**

377 Crouse, Robert. "*Recurrens in te unum*: The Pattern of St. Augustine's *Confessions*." In *Studia Patristica* 14, ed. by Elizabeth Livingstone, 389-92. Berlin: Akademie Verlag, 1976.

Crouse discusses the triformal scheme of ascent (*exteriora, interiora, superiora*) which constitutes the structure of the *Confessions*, and defines the major divisions of the work (Books I-IX, X, XI-XIII).

378 Leigh, David. "Augustine's *Confessions* as a Circular Journey." *Thought: A Review of Culture and Idea* 60 (March 1985): 73-88.

Leigh focuses on the autobiographical books of the *Confessions* (I-IX), claiming that Augustine tells his story in terms of a circular journey of chiasmic form. Books I-IV parallel books VI-IX, with Book V providing the major transition from decline-into-Manicheanism to rise-into-Christianity. The first four books raise questions that are answered in their chiasmic parallels. Augustine probably learned this technique from the *Aeneid* according to Leigh.

379   Levenson, Carl. "Distance and Presence in Augustine's *Confessions*." *Journal of Religion* 65 (October 1985): 500-12.

Based on a Ph.D. dissertation, University of Chicago. Levenson claims that the *Confessions* is structured around four archetypal figures: mother, companion, redeemer, and sage. Each figure is presented twice, first as threatening, then beneficent. Book V is the point of "distance" which marks the shift from threat to benefit. Thus, Books I and IX are about Monica, Books II and VIII about companions, III and VII about Christ, IV and VI about companions again; Book V, finally, is about two sages (Faustus and Ambrose) sandwiched between Augustine's flight from Carthage to Rome.

380   Starnes, Colin. "Saint Augustine on Infancy and Childhood: Commentary on the first Book of Augustine's *Confessions*," *Augustinian Studies* 6 (1975): 15-43.

Starnes offers a trinitarian interpretation of the *Confessions* that solves the unity problem. He claims that the three parts of the text (Books I-IX, X, XI-XIII) correspond to the three persons of the trinity, and that their interconnectedness is likewise analogous to the movement and relations of the persons within the trinity. The commentary on Book I only begins to confirm this thesis. *See also*: **396**.

381   Stephany, William. "Thematic Structure in Augustine's *Confessions*." *Augustinian Studies* 20 (1989): 129-42.

Stephany claims that the first nine books of the *Confessions* are narrated according to an externally imposed structure, specifically a chiasm with Book V at the center. Book IV is paired with Book VI, Book III with VII, and so forth. Stephany thinks that Augustine was motivated to create something proportionately beautiful.

382   Suchocki, Marjorie. "The Symbolic Structure of Augustine's *Confessions*." *Journal of the American Academy of Religion* 50 (September 1982): 365-78.

Suchocki argues that the structure of the *Confessions* centers around two trees (the pear tree in Book II, the fig tree in Book VIII) which correspond symbolically to the two trees in the garden of Eden (the tree of the knowledge of good and evil, and the tree of life). It is this structure, she claims, that accounts for the universal appeal of Augustine's story: he represents how each of us repeats the story of Adam.

383 Torchia, N. Joseph. "St. Augustine's Triadic Interpretation of Iniquity in the *Confessiones.*" In *Collectanea Augustiniana: Augustine, Second Founder of the Faith*, ed. by Joseph Schnaubelt and Frederick Van Fleteren, 159-73. New York: Peter Lang, 1990.

Torchia argues that Augustine's journey to God is organized against the backdrop of a moral triad of vices. The vices are pride, curiosity, and carnal concupiscence.

384 Verheijen, Luc. "The *Confessiones* of Saint Augustine: Two Grids of Composition and of Reading." In *Collectanea Augustiniana: Augustine: Second Founder of the Faith*, ed. by Joseph Schnaubelt and Frederick Van Fleteren, 175-201. New York: Peter Lang, 1990.

Verheijen discerns two grids that determine the structure of the *Confessions*: one for the text as a whole, one for each Book. The text as a whole is organized around Augustine's use of the verb and noun forms of "confession," which reveals a tripartite relationality to God. Each individual book also follows a five part structural pattern.

LANGUAGE AND THE WORD

See also: **073, 114, 121**

385 Bonner, Gerald. "Starting with Oneself; Spiritual Confessions, 4: Saint Augustine's *Confessions.*" *The Expository Times* 101 (March 1990): 163-67.

Bonner believes that it is simplistic to read the *Confessions* as psychological autobiography only. The three-part structure may be confusing to modern readers, but Bonner claims that Augustine follows his autobiographical narrative (ending with his baptism) with a reflection upon Genesis because the healing he experienced at the time of baptism was only a beginning. The further work of God's grace was required, just as it took God six days to complete creation.

386 Chidester, David. "The Symmetry of Word and Light: Perceptual Categories in Augustine's *Confessions.*" *Augustinian Studies* 17 (1986): 119-31.

Chidester believes that the *Confessions* is structured around a balanced presentation of visual and auditory imagery (i.e., Augustine's encounters with divine light and the divine word). The autobiographical narrative, for example, is structured around the symmetry of verbal and visual experiences represented by rhetoric and Manicheism. In general, the *Confessions* moves toward a more pure, unmediated experience of the divine.

387   Flores, Ralph. "Reading and Speech in St. Augustine's *Confessions*." *Augustinian Studies* 6 (1975): 1-13.

Flores argues that the *Confessions* is structured according to Augustine's understanding of language as "reading," which includes the complementary activities of writing, speaking, and exegesis.

388   Vance, Eugene. "Augustine's *Confessions* and the Grammar of Selfhood." *Genre* 6 (1973): 1-28.

Vance believes that Augustine viewed life as a struggle about language. He argues that the *Confessions* begins as autobiography (Books I-X) but ends as biblical commentary (Books XI-XII) because Augustine dramatizes how he is transgressed and, in a sense, violently overcome by the Word. *See also*: **389**.

389   Vance, Eugene. "Augustine's *Confessions* and the Poetics of the Law." *MLN* 93 (1978): 618-34.

Why did Augustine abandon his autobiographical narrative (Books I-IX) in order to interpret Genesis or God's law (Books XI-XIII)? Vance suggests that Augustine passed from narration to exegesis because he wanted God to possess him spiritually/sexually, thereby "circumcising his lips" (freeing him from sin). Augustine's re-wording of God's Word was a redemptive, re-creative exercise. *See also*: **388**.

MOST CRUCIAL BOOK

See also: **107**

390   Callaghan, Thomas. "The Climax of Saint Augustine's *Confessions*." *The Irish Monthly* 49 (November 1941): 511-16.

Callaghan explains the apparent disunity of the *Confessions* (ten books of autobiography, three books of theology) by arguing that the climax comes at the end of Book X, where Augustine speaks of Christ as the mediator between God and humans. Only then is Augustine's restlessness settled, which enables him to turn to more restful or eternal matters.

391   DiLorenzo, Raymond. "Divine Eloquence and the Spiritual World of the *Praedicator*: Book XIII of St. Augustine's *Confessions*." *Augustinian Studies* 16 (1984): 75-88.

DiLorenzo argues that Book XIII is the foundation of all the other books of the *Confessions* because it reflects God's divine plans for the conversion of all creation (of which Augustine's conversion, narrated in the first nine books, is only one instance). He believes the *Confessions* is a story about God more than Augustine.

392 Flood, Emmet. "The Narrative Structure of Augustine's *Confessions*: Time's Quest for Eternity." *International Philosophical Quarterly* 28 (June 1988): 141-62.

Flood disagrees with traditional wisdom that suggests the *Confessions* is a mixture of two kinds of discourse, autobiography (Books I-IX) and theology (Books X-XIII). Instead, he claims that Book X is the central chapter of a unified narrative quest for God. The narrative form was chosen by Augustine in imitation of scripture, and also because it best reflects the temporal qualities of life and language.

393 McMahon, Robert. *Augustine's Prayerful Ascent: An Essay on the Literary Form of the Confessions*. Athens, GA: University of Georgia Press, 1989.

The *Confessions* is a coherently planned (or formed) work, claims McMahon, though part of the plan is to appear planless because it presents itself in the form of a spontaneously delivered oral prayer that moves circuitously and sometimes wanders. Augustine's conclusion in Book 13, an allegory on Genesis, demonstrates this spontaneous, grace-inspired form of the *Confessions*.

394 O'Donnell, James. "Augustine, *Confessions* 10.1.1-10.4.6." *Augustiniana* 29 (1979): 280-303.

This is a line-by-line commentary of the introductory chapters of Book X. O'Donnell tries to show the essential function of Book X in the *Confessions* as a whole.

395 Schimpf, David. *Bible, Christ and Human Beings: The Theological Unity of St. Augustine's Confessions*. Marquette, WI: Marquette University, 1994.

Ph.D. dissertation. Schimpf claims that the unity of the *Confessions* is based upon Augustine's understanding of the two levels of human unity (one in Adam's sin, one in Christ's love). Everything in the *Confessions* points to Book XIII where themes of integration are manifest.

396 Starnes, Colin. "Augustine's Conversion and the Ninth Book of the *Confessions*." In *Augustine: From Rhetor to Theologian*, ed. by Joanne McWilliam, 51-65. Waterloo, ON: Wilfrid Laurier University Press, 1992.

Starnes investigates four issues regarding Book IX: (1) why Augustine included it in the *Confessions*, (2) how it relates to the Cassiciacum *Dialogues*, (3) the vision at Ostia, and (4) why he ended his first confession at this point, only to begin another one of different kind in Book X. He interacts with the best interpreters of the *Confessions*, and defends its integrity. *See also*: **380**.

NARRATIVE PATTERN

See also: 105-06, 160, 163, 189, 307

397   Luman, Richard. "Journeys and Gardens: Narrative Patterns in the *Confessiones* of St. Augustine." In *Collectanea Augustiniana: Augustine, Second Founder of the Faith*, ed. by Joseph Schnaubelt and Frederick Van Fleteren, 141-57. New York: Peter Lang, 1990.

Luman reads the *Confessions* as a narrative shaped by common storytelling devices that allude to other stories while not necessarily compromising the historical integrity of the text. As journey, the *Confessions* is a hybrid story comparable to the *Odyssey*, *Aeneid*, and *Epic of Gilgamesh*. The numerous garden scenes invariably depict a conversion of some sort.

398   Poland, Lynn. "Invocation as Interruption in Augustine's *Confessions*." In *Morphologies of Faith: Essays in Religion and Culture in Honor of Nathan A. Scott, Jr.*, ed. by Mary Gerhart and A. Yu, 343-57. American Academy of Religion Studies in Religion, 59. Atlanta: Scholars Press, 1990.

Poland distinguishes two types of readers for the *Confessions*: the insider who understands Augustine's invocations to God as intimate conversation, and the outsider who understands the invocations as interruptions. She argues that these interruptions attest to the necessary conditions of narrative structure.

RHETORICAL ANALYSIS

See also: 093, 108, 125, 386-87, 393

399   Boyle, Marjorie O'Rourke. "The Prudential Augustine: The Virtuous Structure and Sense of his *Confessions*." In *Recherches Augustiniennes* XXII, ed. by J. Pius-Camps, et al., 129-50. Paris: Études Augustiniennes, 1987.

Boyle argues that the *Confessions* is composed in classical Ciceronian fashion. It is encomium about the good and just God; its rhetoric is epideictic, meaning that it honors virtue. Augustine was concerned with the virtue of prudence (or knowledge of good and evil), according to Boyle. The three parts of prudence (memory, intelligence, foresight) determine the three parts of the *Confessions*: Books I-IX, memory; Book X, intelligence; Books XI-XIII, foresight. *See also*: 002.

400   Johnson, Donovan. "Story and Design in Book VIII of Augustine's *Confessions*." *Biography: An Interdisciplinary Quartery* 14 (Winter 1991): 39-60.

Johnson examines the four stories Augustine narrates in Book VIII in order to demonstate how he achieves his rhetorical purpose, which is to persuade the reader to take up the stance of faith. Augustine presents himself as a positive and negative model of the Christian paradigm of "lost and found."

401 Siebach, James. "Rhetorical Strategies in Book One of St. Augustine's *Confessions*." *Augustinian Studies* 25 (1995): 93-108.

Siebach argues that the *Confessions* are structured around a proof for God's existence that implicitly answers the question about how metaphysical realms of being and becoming are related. Based upon rhetorical analysis of Book I, Siebach concludes that the purpose of Augustine's "confession" is union with God.

STAGES OF GROWTH

See also: **085, 149, 360, 377**

402 Crosson, Frederick. "Philosophy, Religion and Faith." In *Immateriality: Proceedings of the American Catholic Philosophical Association*, 52, ed. by George McLean, 168-76. Washington: American Catholic Philosophical Association, 1978.

Crosson investigates how philosophy, religion (or mythological story telling), and faith enable us to make sense of the world as a whole. He turns to the *Confessions* in order to illustrate how Augustine is able to maintain all three points of view. *See also*: **403**.

403 Crosson, Frederick. "Religion and Faith in St. Augustine's *Confessions*." In *Rationality and Religious Belief*, ed. by C. F. Delaney, 152-68. University of Notre Dame Studies in the Philosophy of Religion, 1. Notre Dame, IN: University of Notre Dame Press, 1979.

Crosson argues that the *Confessions* are structured according to a sequence of phases that Augustine passes through. First is the phase of religious mythology, then philosophy, and finally biblical faith. *See also*: **402**.

404 Doull, James. "What is Augustinian '*Sapientia*'?" *Dionysius* 12 (December 1988): 61-67.

In a reading of the *Confessions* that takes into account each part, Doull sets forth Augustine's *sapientia* (science of God) in its threefold movement (from awareness of God's immutable distance, to awareness of God's eternal presence, to intimate encounter with God in Christ).

405   Dutton, Marsha. "'When I Was a Child': Spiritual Infancy and God's Maternity in Augustine's *Confessiones.*" In *Collectanea Augustiniana: Augustine: Second Founder of the Faith*, ed. by Joseph Schnaubelt and Frederick Van Fleteren, 113-40. New York: Peter Lang, 1990.

Dutton reads the *Confessions* as documenting Augustine's spiritual maturing process. In his spiritual infancy, God is seen as a mother and Jesus as the mother's milk. In his spiritual maturity, reached in the vision at Ostia, Augustine is able to wean himself from the mother's milk, and retire the metaphor of God's maternity. This shift from infancy to maturity demarcates the difference between the first nine books of the *Confessions*, and the last four.

406   Earl, James. "The Typology of Spiritual Growth in Augustine's *Confessions.*" *Notre Dame English Journal* 13 (Spring 1981): 13-28.

Earl means two things by "typology": a system of relations among historical events, and a system of relations between events and ideas. He employs these definitions in order to demonstrate how the *Confessions* fuses history, philosophy, and scripture into a unified structural system.

407   Hanson-Smith, Elizabeth. "Augustine's *Confessions*: The Concrete Referent." *Philosophy and Literature* 2 (Fall 1978): 176-89.

Hanson-Smith looks to Augustine's earlier work, *de quantitate animae*, for a structural model of the *Confessions*. The seven steps of the soul's ascent to God sketched in that text are translated into the narrative of the *Confessions*. Studying them side by side reveals the philosophical premises undergirding Augustine's educational journey.

408   Harpham, Geoffrey. *The Ascetic Imperative in Culture and Criticism.* Chicago: University of Chicago Press, 1987.

Based upon a reading of early Christianity, Harpham develops a theory of asceticism as binary resistance that underlies all cultures. He employs his resistance theory of asceticism to interpret contemporary culture and interpretation theory. In Part 2 of his book, Harpham employs Jaspers's three stages of the soul (from world orientation, to illumination, to metaphysics) to interpret the three successive parts of Augustine's *Confessions* (from autobiography, to philosophy, to exegesis). He claims that the modes of Augustine's writing are phases in an evolution toward perfect ascesis or self-renunciation.

409   Martin, Thomas. "A Journey of Faith: The *Confessions* of St. Augustine." *Review for Religious* 39 (September 1980): 651-57.

Martin employs an Old Testament model of the journey of faith to interpret the *Confessions*: first comes God's call, then rejection of the call, conversion, and finally covenant with God.

410   Pincherle, Alberto. "The *Confessions* of St. Augustine: A Reappraisal." *Augustinian Studies* 7 (1976): 119-33.

Pincherle explains how Augustine came to write the *Confessions* as he did by referring to his experiences and struggles of that time. His efforts to study the Bible, at Simplicianus's urging, figure prominently in the structure of the text and the inclusion of books XI-XIII.

411   Shanzer, Danuta. "Latent Narrative Patterns, Allegorical Choices, and Literary Unity in Augustine's *Confessions*." *Vigiliae Christianae* 46 (March 1992): 40-56.

Shanzer argues that the presence of literary patterns and allusions in the *Confessions* (conversion in a garden, for example) does not mean that Augustine reconstructed the facts of his life in a deceiving fashion. It is possible that the literary pattern influenced the initial behavior as well as the interpretation of it. She believes that the unity of the *Confessions* might be part of such a pattern: Augustine's autobiography becomes more and more scripture-like as he makes progress in his search for scriptural meaning.

412   Starnes, Colin. *Augustine's Conversion: A Guide to the Argument of Confessions I-IX.* Waterloo, ON: Wilfrid Laurier University Press, 1990.

In this commentary on the first part of the *Confessions*, Starnes uncovers Augustine's argument, that is, the reasons why he moved from one position to the next in the process of becoming a Catholic Christian. He tries to demonstrate how the *Confessions* is more than autobiography; it represents the unique claims of Christianity upon all ancient people.

THEMATIC UNITY

See also: **144, 328**

413   Cooper, John. "Why did Augustine Write Books XI-XIII of the *Confessions*?" *Augustinian Studies* 2 (1971): 37-46.

Cooper believes that there are two key themes in the *Confessions* (the soul's attraction to God; the majesty of God), and it is their linkage that constitutes the unity of the text. Augustine explores the first theme in books I-IX, and the second theme in books XI-XIII. In both cases, his purpose is to answer basic human questions about the meaning of life.

414   Grant, Patrick. "Redeeming the Time: The *Confessions* of St. Augustine." In *By Things Seen: Reference and Recognition in Medieval Thought*, ed. by David Jeffrey, 21-32. Ottawa: University of Ottawa Press, 1979.

Grant comments upon several critical problems in his reading of the *Confessions*, chiefly its baffling structure. In part, the difficulty stems from Augustine's attempt to write about past events while attempting to resolve issues that he was currently facing (Manicheism, for example). Nevertheless, Grant thinks the coordinating principle of the *Confessions* is Augustine's theory of fallen humanity and temporal redemption.

415   Huddlestun, Bernard. *Augustine's Confessions X-XI*. Washington: Catholic University of America, 1972.

Ph.D. dissertation. Huddlestun offers a paragraph by paragraph commentary on two philosophically significant books of the *Confessions*. He draws two negative conclusions: (1) memory and time are not the leading themes of these books, as is commonly thought; and (2) categorizing the *Confessions* as autobiographical, psychological, and so forth, overlooks its thematic unity, which is why modern interpreters have such a problem with the unity of the text.

416   Nygren, Andre. "The Meaning and Structure of St. Augustine's *Confessions*." *The Lutheran Church Quarterly* 21 (July 1948): 148-55.

Nygren reviews German scholarship on the unity question, then proposes that the content of the *Confessions* is the key to understanding its literary structure. The whole work revolves around the "restless heart" theme.

417   O'Connell, Robert. "The Riddle of Augustine's *Confessions*: A Plotinian Key." *International Philosophical Quarterly* 4 (September 1964): 327-72.

O'Connell articulates what he takes to be the meaning (or purpose) of the *Confessions*, which then enables him to solve the three nettling problems of modern *Confessions* criticism (unity of the text, historicity of the conversion, sources of Neoplatonic influence). Augustine's purpose, he claims, is to retell the tale of Adam's (humanity's) fall and return using both biblical and Plotinian terminology. This article previews *St. Augustine's Confessions: The Odyssey of Soul* (**215**).

418   Rocklage, Mary. *A Thematic Analysis of the Imagery in the Confessions of St. Augustine*. St. Louis: St. Louis University, 1965.

Ph.D. dissertation. Rocklage studies the visual imagery of the *Confessions* that pertains to the theme of rest and unrest. She notes how images of rest increase as the text progresses, which helps to establish a sense of unity.

419 Steinhauser, Kenneth. "The Literary Unity of the *Confessions*." In *Augustine: From Rhetor to Theologian*, ed. by Joanne McWilliam, 15-30. Waterloo, ON: Wilfrid Laurier University Press, 1992.

Steinhauser carefully analyzes previous scholarship, then proposes a new composite solution to the unity question. He draws three conclusions: that Augustine's own description of the *Confessions* must be respected (a record of his search for truth and conversion to Christianity); that the thirteen books are complete as they now stand; and that the final structure of the *Confessions* does not represent an artificial rearrangement of previously composed pieces.

420 Tavard, George. "The Problem of Space and Time in the *Confessions* of St. Augustine." *Dialogue and Alliance* 2 (Spring 1988): 49-55.

Tavard believes the *Confessions* is structured around two foci, space and time. In Book I of the *Confessions*, Augustine raises spatial questions (where is God?); in Book XI, he raises questions about eternity and time (what was God doing before he created the world?). Answering these questions enabled Augustine to confess his Christian knowledge of God.

9

Theological Interpretation

DOCTRINAL DEBATE

See also: **057, 063, 174, 179, 186, 190, 200, 203, 267, 311, 315, 440**

421 Fenn, Richard. "Magic in Language and Ritual: Notes on Augustine's *Confessions*." *Journal for the Scientific Study of Religion* 25 (March 1986): 77-91.

Fenn thinks that Augustine attempted to replace the magic of ritual with language, particularly the doctrine of predestination. This was an unfortunate turn for Christianity because language (even language like Augustine's, larded with scripture and mythology) can only talk about relieving us from life's harms.

422 Kaufman, Peter. "The Lesson of Conversion: A Note on the Question of Continuity in Augustine's Understanding of Grace and Human Will." *Augustinian Studies* 11 (1980): 49-64.

Kaufman believes that the lesson of Augustine's conversion, first intimated in *de libero arbitrio* and the *Confessions*, is fully declared forty years later in the anti-Pelagian treatise, *de gratia et libero arbitrio*. The lesson is that human effort and divine grace are necessary in the effort to make a righteous and robust will.

423 Manville, Brook. "Donatism and St. Augustine: The *Confessions* of a 4th Century Bishop." *Augustinian Studies* 8 (1977): 125-37.

Manville claims that Augustine wrote the *Confessions* in response to the Donatism schism that was threatening the African Church at that time. Issues raised by the Donatists (the role of church in society, the role of a bishop's personal life in his church responsibilities) provided a focus for Augustine's self-examination.

424   O'Connell, Robert. "Alypius' 'Apollinarianism' at Milan." *Revue des Études Augustiniennes* 13 (1967): 209-10.

O'Connell briefly contradicts the mistaken view that Alypius's understanding of Christ, as portrayed in Book VII of the *Confessions*, is Apollinarian (believing that Christ had no human soul).

GOD TALK

See also: **005, 059, 067, 089, 099, 206, 271, 274, 284, 299, 376, 384, 391, 398-99, 401, 404, 413, 420, 466**

425   Bradley, Ritamary. "Naming God in St. Augustine's *Confessions*." *Thomist* 17 (April 1954): 186-96.

Bradley studies Augustine's discussion of God's attributes in the final four books of the *Confessions*. She claims that Augustine was able to conflate Neoplatonic notions of the divine (eternity, unity, immutability, beauty) with the "I Am Who Am" definition from Exodus.

426   O'Connell, Robert. "The God of St. Augustine's Imagination." *Thought: A Review of Culture and Idea* 57 (1982): 30-40.

O'Connell explores the many images of God (warming wind, father, doctor, nurse, mother) pertaining to Augustine's use of the term *fovere* in the *Confessions*. Everything earthly speaks of God's omnipresence; Augustine's multivocal response, according to O'Connell, is properly imaginative.

427   O'Donnell, James. "Augustine's Idea of God." *Augustinian Studies* 25 (1994): 25-36.

O'Donnell meditates on a passage from the *Confessions* in which Augustine expresses an inability to say anything clearly about God even though the experience of God is central to everything else that he says.

428   O'Loughlin, Thomas. "Knowing God and Knowing the Cosmos: Augustine's Legacy of Tension." *Irish Philosophical Journal* 6 (1989): 27-58.

O'Loughlin studies three works of Augustine's (*Confessiones, de genesi ad litteram*, and *de doctrina christiana*) in order to explore the sources of medieval cosmology, which entails a basic tension concerning the cosmos: on the one hand, the cosmos is God's creation, therefore admirable; on the other hand, the cosmos is as nothing compared to God. According to O'Loughlin, this tension is a result of Augustine's attempt to synthesize biblical and classical cultural traditions.

429 Steinhauser, Kenneth. "Creation in the Image of God according to Augustine's *Confessions.*" *Patristic and Byzantine Review* 7 (1988): 199-204.

Believing that the Neoplatonist influence on the young Augustine has been over-emphasized, Steinhauser argues that a Manichean residue can be discerned in the *imago dei* theology of the *Confessions*.

NATURE OF THEOLOGY

See also: **063, 066, 071, 093, 123-24, 143, 185, 188, 196, 204, 254, 259, 260, 262, 298, 302, 304, 317, 373, 380**

430 Burke, Kenneth. *The Rhetoric of Religion: Studies in Logology*. Berkeley, CA: University of California Press, 1961.

Burke studies theology (words about God) in order to gain insight about logology (words about words). He assumes that what theologians say about God is comparable to what might be said about words, since both God and language share formal characteristics. The theological text Burke employs in this rhetorical experiment is the *Confessions* (the story of a rhetorician who became a theologian). *See also*: **432**.

431 Burrell, David. "Reading the *Confessions* of Augustine: An Exercise in Theological Understanding." *Journal of Religion* 50 (1970): 327-51.

Burrell believes that the *Confessions* is primarily an exercise in theological understanding that, when studied appropriately, can improve the reader's understanding. The reader must be critical and self-reflective, willing to enter into the world of the text. Ultimately what we learn from the *Confessions*, according to Burrell, is how religious discourse actually becomes part of lived experience.

432 Freccero, John. "Logology: Burke on St. Augustine." In *Representing Kenneth Burke*, ed. by Hayden White and Margaret Brose, 52-67. Selected papers from the English Institute, 6. Baltimore: Johns Hopkins University Press, 1982.

Freccero offers a concise, complimentary review of Burke's *The Rhetoric of Religion* (**430**), which investigates the *Confessions* as a (theological) language system in pursuit of absolute unity and perfection.

433 Harvey, John. *Moral Theology of the Confessions of Saint Augustine*. Studies in Sacred Theology, 2d series, 55. Washington: Catholic University of America Press, 1951.

Ph.D. dissertation. Harvey investigates the moral teaching of the Confessions, which he summarizes under ten headings: (1) God is the goal of human life, (2) infused charity must be the bond of union between friends, (3) humility is the foundation of charity, (4) continence must be prayed for, (5) rationalization is wishful thinking, (6) a divided will results from the lack of a dominant aim in life, (7) bad habit begins as rebellion against God, (8) pride motivates the sinner to choose creature over creator, (9) each kind of sin brings its special punishment, and (10) the remedies of sin are good example, scripture, and grace.

434   Lehrberger, James. "*Intelligo-ut-credam*: St. Augustine's *Confessions*." *Thomist* 52 (January 1988): 23-39.

Lehrberger argues that the *Confessions* demonstrates how reason alone, without revelation, is capable of assessing religious claims to be revealed truth. Accordingly, reason provides a negative norm for faith. Lehrberger explores Augustine's criteria for such evaluation, especially as developed in his discussion of Manicheism.

435   Mallard, William. *Language and Love: Introducing Augustine's Religious Thought Through the Confessions Story*. University Park, PA: Pennsylvania State University Press, 1994.

Mallard provides a theological meditation on Books I-IX of the *Confessions* that anticipates the major topics of Augustine's mature theology: the goodness of creation; the struggles of the human will; Christian identity in a strange world; and the relationship between reason and authority. He claims that Augustine's creationist solution to the problems of restlessness and alienation can still work today.

436   O'Leary, Joseph. *Questioning Back: The Overcoming of Metaphysics in Christian Tradition*. Minneapolis: Winston Press, 1985.

What does fidelity to the Christian tradition entail today? O'Leary claims that we must counter-read the morose, introspective metaphysics that has dominated faith since the time of Augustine. He offers deconstructive hints on how to read the *Confessions* so that we might appreciate the less confident, searching man of faith who had not yet imposed an absolute (and, to a modern sensibility, mistaken) order on his life and faith.

437   Olmsted, Wendy. "Philosophical Inquiry and Religious Transformation in Boethius's *The Consolation of Philosophy* and Augustine's *Confessions*." *Journal of Religion* 69 (January 1989): 14-35.

Olmstead attempts to say what "religion" means by reading two classic texts for which religious life is problematic. Religion is problematic in the *Confessions* because there are so many candidates with answers to Augustine's questions; it is

problematic in the *Consolation* because Boethius seeks answers to religious
questions from natural philosophy alone. Olmsted argues that both are religious
texts, though different, because (1) they originate in basic existential questions,
and (2) they attempt to enact change through a dialogic process.

438 Stroup, George. *The Promise of Narrative Theology: Recovering the
Gospel in the Church.* Atlanta: John Knox Press, 1981.

Stroup believes that Christian identity is in crisis, and that narrative (or
experiential) theology might help alleviate the problem. He employs
Augustine's *Confessions* in order to demonstrate how the narrative structure of
Christian faith (and revelation) becomes real in the confrontation between
community and convert.

439 TeSelle, Sallie McFague. *Speaking in Parables: A Study in Metaphor and
Theology.* Philadelphia: Fortress Press, 1975.

In order to make theology relevant, it must be made more personal or parabolic
according to TeSelle. She focuses upon personal literature (parables, poems,
autobiographies, letters, novels) as an important resource for theology. She
briefly interprets the *Confessions* as illustrating the principles of her parabolic
theology, chiefly the embodiment of language in a way of life.

440 Van Fleteren, Frederick. "Authority and Reason, Faith and Understanding
in the Thought of St. Augustine." *Augustinian Studies* 4 (1973): 33-71.

Van Fleteren charts the progress of Augustine's thinking about authority and
reason from the time of his earliest writings until his death. The *Confessions*
figure prominently in this study because they chronicle Augustine's Manichean
experience, where the debate between authority and reason originates. As a
Manichean, Augustine tended to place reason above authority. That order is
reversed with his conversion.

SEARCH FOR TRUTH

See also: **019, 032, 042, 056, 085, 105, 108, 129, 135, 191, 199, 201-02, 222,
238, 329, 336, 362, 400, 419**

441 Crawford, Dan. "Intellect and Will in Augustine's *Confessions*."
Religious Studies 24 (Summer 1988): 291-302.

Crawford reviews Augustine's search for truth in the *Confessions*, determining in
what sense his search was satisfied by the knowledge of God. Then he
extrapolates a theory of will from Augustine's conversion scene.

442   DiLorenzo, Raymond. *"Non Pie Quaerunt*: Rhetoric, Dialectic, and the Discovery of the True in Augustine's *Confessions." Augustinian Studies* 14 (1983): 117-28.

DiLorenzo claims that Augustine created a new style of philosophising that subordinated dialectical reason to confessional rhetoric, thus linking scientia to sapientia. The problem with previous philosophies, for Augustine, was that they did not seek truth piously (*non pie quareunt*). In Augustine's philosophy, wisdom is piety, and piety is confession to God.

443   Ferrari, Leo. "The 'Food of Truth' in Augustine's *Confessions." Augustinian Studies* 9 (1978): 1-14.

Ferrari examines the rich variety of alimentary allusions that spice the *Confessions* when viewed as the search of a starved soul for the divine food of truth. He observes the distinction between sexual lust, which Augustine conquered upon conversion, and concupiscence for food, which Augustine found more recalcitrant. *See also*: **308**.

444   Miles, Margaret. "Vision: The Eye of the Body and the Eye of the Mind in Saint Augustine's *de trinitate* and *Confessions." Journal of Religion* 63 (April 1983): 125-42.

Miles demonstrates how Augustine's understanding of physical vision informs his spiritual efforts to see God and soul as they are. She undertakes this project in order to correct traditional views of Augustine's theory of illumination, which overlook the necessity of human effort in order to see properly.

SIN

See also: **021, 060, 094, 112, 141, 214, 224, 231, 276, 306, 343, 389, 395, 414, 417, 457**

445   D'Souza, Dinesh. "Augustine's *Confessions." Columbia* 68 (August 1988): 17-18.

Reflecting upon the *Confessions*, D'Souza indicates that its value for today pertains to the illumination of sin (which is often disregarded).

446   Ferrari, Leo. "Symbols of Sinfulness in Book II of Augustine's 'Confession.'" *Augustinian Studies* 2 (1971): 93-104.

Ferrari explores the seemingly exaggerative significance of the pear tree incident in Augustine's life. He focuses upon the wilderness and peregrination symbols that Augustine employs in Book II as he recounts the sinfulness of his youth. *See also*: **457**.

447   Mann, William. "The Theft of the Pears." *Apeiron: A Journal for Ancient Philosophy and Science* 12 (1978): 51-58.

Mann investigates Book II of the *Confessions*, wondering why Augustine chose such a trivial example of sin (stealing pears), and why he was (or should have been) puzzled by his explanation of the theft. He claims that Augustine took the theft seriously because it was a case of sinning for the sake of sinning, and he claims that Augustine's explanation is unsatisfactory because evil has inscrutable origins.

448   Mann, William. "Dreams of Immorality." *Philosophy: The Journal of the Royal Institute of Philosophy* 58 (July 1983): 378-85.

Mann defends three doctrines that support Augustine's view (expressed in Book X of the *Confessions*) that it is possible to sin while sleeping. He writes in support of Matthews's earlier article on the topic (**449**).

449   Matthews, Gareth. "On Being Immoral in a Dream." *Philosophy: The Journal of the Royal Institute of Philosophy* 56 (January 1981): 47-54.

Matthews mentions two Cartesian dream problems in Augustine's thought, then focuses upon the second one which stems from a passage in Book X of the *Confessions*. In the *Confessions* passage, Augustine claims not to be responsible for wet dreams. Matthews tries to articulate what kind of "dream self" Augustine is proposing when he comes to the no fault conclusion. He believes Augustine is being inconsistent. *See also*: **448**.

450   Miles, Margaret. "The Body and Human Values in Augustine of Hippo." In *Grace, Politics and Desire: Essays on Augustine*, ed. by Hugo Meynell, 55-67. Calgary: University of Calgary Press, 1990.

Relying upon the *Confessions* and *City of God*, Miles investigates Augustine's key concept of concupiscence. She claims that we misunderstand Augustine when we blame him for disparaging the body, even though his sense of life as flawed is harsh.

451   Miles, Margaret. "Infancy, Parenting, and Nourishment in Augustine's *Confessions*." *Journal of the American Academy of Religion* 50 (Spring 1982): 349-64.

Miles attends to the question of how Augustine came to make sense of the concupiscence that manifested itself in his earliest recollections. She interprets his conversion as a parental switch: God becomes the source of true nourishment as the obsessive desires associated with childhood and earthly parenting are displaced.

452   O'Brien, William. "Toward Understanding Original Sin in Augustine's *Confessions.*" *Thought: A Review of Culture and Idea* 49 (December 1974): 436-46.

O'Brien contends that the modern reader must attend to Augustine's understanding of original sin in order to appreciate the prayerful form of the *Confessions.* Original sin, for Augustine, symbolizes a region of dark separation from God that is part of every person's historical destiny.

453   Ramirez, J. Roland. "Demythologizing Augustine as Great Sinner." *Augustinian Studies* 12 (1981): 61-88.

Augustine's claim to be a great sinner in the *Confessions* is exaggerated according to Ramirez, who examines the issue according to the standards of ancient times. Ramirez does not think his assessment damages Augustine's truthfulness or reputation because a mystical sensibility makes Augustine more sensitive to transgressions of divine love.

454   Rigby, Paul. *Original Sin in Augustine's Confessions.* Ottawa: University of Ottawa Press, 1987.

Rigby argues that Augustine's doctrine of original sin is foundational, not derivative, for his theological anthropology. The issue of Augustine's motives for developing this doctrine is key; Rigby reveals the psychological dynamic entailed in Augustine's formulation of original sin.

455   Schlabach, Gerald. "Friendship as Adultery: Social Reality and Sexual Metaphor in Augustine's Doctrine of Original Sin." *Augustinian Studies* 23 (1992): 125-47.

Augustine's doctrine of original sin is entrenched in sexuality issues that are irrelevant today. Relying upon Books IV-VI of the *Confessions,* Schlabach articulates what an Augustinian theory of original sin would look like if transmission were social rather than sexual. The instrumental use of others is the essential problem, not sex.

USE OF SCRIPTURE

See also: **017, 019, 058, 070, 115, 121-22, 132, 140, 142, 147, 154-56, 179, 186, 197, 200, 207, 213, 219, 227, 242, 305, 359, 382, 385, 388-89, 392-93, 406, 409-11, 428, 441**

456   Burns, Paul. "Augustine's Distinctive Use of the Psalms in the *Confessions*: The Role of Music and Recitation." *Augustinian Studies* 24 (1993): 133-46.

Psalms are cited more than two hundred times in the *Confessions*, though rarely in an organized exegetical manner. Burns claims that it is Augustine's memory steeped in daily recitation and singing of the Psalms which influenced the way they function in his autobiography.

457 Ferrari, Leo. "The Arboreal Polarization in Augustine's *Confessions*." *Revue des Études Augustiniennes* 25 (1979): 35-46.

Ferrari defends the thesis that the *Confessions* is polarized between good and evil as symbolized by two trees. The fig tree under which he experienced conversion represents goodness, while the pear tree from which he stole as a boy represents evil. Ferrari argues that Augustine borrowed this rhetorical strategy from the Bible, which is itself "polarized" between the tree of Adam's sin and the tree upon which Christ was crucified. *See also*: **382, 446**.

458 Ferrari, Leo. "Augustine's 'Discovery' of Paul (*Confessions* 7.21.27)." *Augustinian Studies* 22 (1991): 37-61.

Ferrari explains how, in Book VII of the *Confessions*, Augustine leads the reader to believe that he has just discovered the writings of Paul. According to Ferrari, it was not that Augustine discovered Paul, but that he was finally able to overcome a post-Manichean bias against Paul (a Manichean favorite).

459 Ferrari, Leo. "From Pagan Literature to the Pages of the Holy Scriptures: Augustine's *Confessions* as Exemplary Propaedeutic." In *Kerygma und Logos: Beiträge zu den geistesgeschichtlichen Beziehungen zwischen Antike und Christentum*, ed. by Adolf Ritter, 173-182. Festschrift für Carl Andresen zum 70. Geburtstag. Göttingen: Vandenhoeck and Ruprecht, 1979.

Ferrari reads the *Confessions* as a book about books, commenting upon Augustine's movement from the literature of paganism that he learned in school to the holy scriptures that he embraced upon becoming Christian. Unlike many others from that era, according to Ferrari, Augustine never rejected the value of non-Christian literature.

460 Ferrari, Leo. "Isaiah and the Early Augustine." In *Collectanea Augustiniana: Mélanges T. J. Van Bavel*, ed. by Bernard Bruning, M. Lamberigts, and J. Van Houtem, 739-56. Leuven: University Press, 1990.

In Book IX of the *Confessions*, Augustine mentions that Ambrose encouraged him to study the prophet Isaiah. Ferrari analyzes the incident and determines what Isaiahan texts contributed to Augustine's early writings.

461 Ferrari, Leo. "The Theme of the Prodigal Son in Augustine's *Confessions*." *Recherches Augustiniennes* 12 (1977): 105-18.

Ferrari investigates Augustine's allusions to the prodigal son parable in the *Confessions*. He relies upon other writings of Augustine's in order to appreciate his interpretation of the parable.

462   Ferrari, Leo. "Young Augustine: Both Catholic and Manachee." *Augustinian Studies* 25 (1995): 109-28.

When did Augustine's Manicheism expire? Perhaps not as soon as the *Confessions* leads us to believe according to Ferrari. He focuses upon two textual problems: (1) the absence of biblical citations to a Pauline text that Ambrose preached about and that supposedly cleared up Augustine's Manichean confusions; and (2) Augustine's continued aversion to the prophet Isaiah (a Manichean trait) even after he claims to have left the sect.

463   Lawless, George. "Interior Peace in the *Confessions* of St. Augustine." *Revue des Études Augustiniennes* 26 (1980): 45-61.

Studying passages from the *Confessions* that include *pax* and related words, Lawless evaluates the biblical and philosophical evidence for Augustine's pursuit of peace. He concludes that the biblical motifs of creation and sabbath are the most determinative influences on Augustine's quest for peace.

464   Spicer, Malcolm. "AD 386 - AD 1986: The Conversion of St. Augustine." *Canadian Catholic Review* 4 (October 1986): 6-12.

Spicer meditates on the *Confessions* as a prayer for help in understanding the first sentence of the Bible (Gen. 1:1). The real conversion story being told is Augustine's life-long conversion to scripture.

465   Sundén, Hjalmar. "Saint Augustine and the Psalter in the Light of Role-Psychology." *Journal for the Scientific Study of Religion* 26 (1987): 375-82.

Sundén claims that Augustine's prayerful use of the psalms enabled him to experience God's presence. This contradicts the prevalent view that the *Confessions* marks the highwater mark of Augustine's tutelage to Plotinus, who did not believe in prayer.

466   Sylvester-Johnson, John. *The Psalms in the Confessions of Augustine.* Southern Baptist Theological Seminary, 1981.

Ph.D. dissertation. Sylvester-Johnson analyzes Augustine's developing use of the Psalms in his thinking about God, the human condition, and the divine-human encounter. He claims that the *Confessions* are an act of worship modeled upon the praise of the Psalms.

467 Teske, Roland. "'*Homo Spiritualis*' in the *Confessions* of St. Augustine." In *Augustine: From Rhetor to Theologian*, ed. by Joanne McWilliam, 67-76. Waterloo, ON: Wilfrid Laurier University Press, 1992.

Teske interprets Augustine's use of St. Paul's concept of the spiritual person in a specific text from Book XIII of the *Confessions*. He claims that Augustine's use of St. Paul is more Neoplatonic than Pauline.

468 Van Winden, Jacobus. "Once Again *Caelum Caeli*: Is Augustine's Argument in *Confessions* XII Consistent?" In *Collectanea Augustiniana: Mélanges T. J. Van Bavel*, ed. by Bernard Bruning, M. Lamberigts, and J. Van Houtem., 905-11. Leuven: University Press, 1990.

Van Winden responds to an earlier French discussion concerning the meaning of *caelum caeli* (spiritual creation) in Book XII of the *Confessions*. Contrary to the earlier thesis, Van Winden claims that Augustine meant "spiritual creation" in its formed (not unformed) state. That means there could not be a spiritual being who was not already turned toward God. In that case, Augustine's interpretation of Genesis 1.1 in books XI-XII is consistent.

Index of Authors and Editors

Notations preceded by "p." or "pp." refer to page numbers in the preface and introductory chapter. All other notations refer to entry numbers for items listed in the annotated bibliography.

Index of Titles

Notations preceded by "p." or "pp." refer to page numbers in the preface and introductory chapter. All other notations refer to entry numbers for items listed in the annotated bibliography.

Index of Subjects

Notations preceded by "p." or "pp." refer to page numbers in the preface and introductory chapter. All other notations refer to entry numbers for items listed in the annotated bibliography.

About the Author

RICHARD SEVERSON is a Reference Librarian at Marylhurst College in Marylhurst, Oregon. His first book, *Time, Death, and Eternity*, was published in 1995.

ISBN 0-313-29995-1

90000>

EAN

9 780313 299957

HARDCOVER BAR CODE